The Good
Relationship
Guide

The Good Relationship Guide

how to understand and improve male-female relationships

Dr Maryon Tysoe

PIATKUS

301.41

306.7

First published in 1995
by Judy Piatkus (Publishers) Ltd of
5 Windmill Street, London W1P 1HF

The moral rights of the author have been asserted

*A catalogue record for this book is
available from the British Library*

ISBN 0–7499–1548–X Hbk
ISBN 0–7499–1481–5 Pbk

Designed by Sue Ryall

Typeset by Datix International Limited, Bungay, Suffolk
Printed and bound in Great Britain by Biddles Ltd,
Guildford & King's Lynn

0749 915 48x 1309

Contents

Introduction

Developing and keeping a good relationship is probably one of the hardest things human beings ever have to do. What is extraordinary is that we are all woefully unprepared for it. We leave school knowing more about our reproductive organs than about the skills of relationships. Somehow, we're just supposed to 'know' how to do it.

We all do our best to learn by experience. We gossip avidly about each other's relationships. We watch them like hawks. We scavenge through culture for clues. We read novels, struggle not to cough in the big renunciation scene of the latest adultery play, and spill popcorn in our excitement when woman gets man in the new blockbuster film. We practise on a few relationships of our own, boosting the share price of Kleenex along the way.

The trouble is that there are no rules about relationships. There is no easy 'get your relationships right while you sleep' audiotape. No 'ten steps to perfect happiness'. No 'three keys to eternal love'.

Nevertheless, humanity is not quite as ignorant as it used to be about such matters. A good deal of knowledge has been building up over the years. It has, however, been developing in a rather inaccessible place: inside the covers of academic psychology journals lurk the results of thousands of research studies conducted by psychologists.

1

The aim of this book is to look closely at how relationships work, informed by psychological research. Many books about relationships are based on therapists' experiences with clients in difficulties, and the conclusions they draw from these experiences. I am a social psychologist, not a therapist. I take the view that carefully-controlled scientific studies and experiments can be of immense value, and that findings with a solid research backing are not the common knowledge that they should be.

I want to use these findings to address the difficulties that most of us face. It's transparently obvious that male–female love relationships are in chaos in the 1990s, and it's a rare creature – I'm certainly not one of them – who hasn't tear-soaked a fair number of pillowcases in her time. You only need to look at the divorce statistics and the faces of miserably married friends – and of single ones suffering anguish in the relationship department – to see the scale of the problem. (I use the words 'marriage' and 'divorce' frequently in this book because much research has been done on married couples and divorce. But you can also take these words as shorthand for 'long-term live-in committed relationships' and their break-up.)

The key to improving matters lies, in my view, in increasing our knowledge of how relationships work. It's time for some smart love. So if you're in a relationship, but afraid that something will go wrong; in a relationship, and pretty sure something already has; or you've had your share of relationship break-ups, and want to give yourself a better chance of a good relationship next time; then this guide is for you.

1

Choosing

We've all done it. You catch sight of a man across a crowded room and you say, 'Look at *him*!'

And the girlfriend you're with does look at him. 'Excuse me?' she says. 'You mean the one with the ginger hair and the rocket-shaped nose and the bandy legs and the ears like dinghy sails?'

'That's the one,' you say, gazing at him with racing heart and weakened knees.

'Well,' she says, gazing at you sidelong and wondering how many glasses of vile plonk you've drunk, 'he doesn't do anything for me.'

So here we are, at the mysterious beginning of that difficult 'relationship' business.

SNAP JUDGEMENTS

When you set eyes on a new person, you make a lot of snap judgements – in particular, on whether or not he is physically attractive. Within each society, people tend to agree on who is objectively good-looking and who isn't (which is not the same as how *fanciable* he is to each of those people). There's evidence that we can make this judgement in 0.1 of a second. The trouble is, doing so activates a deeply held 'what is beautiful is good' stereotype.

The 'good-looking' stereotype

After sexism, racism and ageism, the time is ripe for the concept of lookism. We irrationally favour good-looking people – which is great for them, of course. Not, however, so great for all those who really don't care to catch sight of themselves in a full-length mirror.

A Yale University psychologist, Alan Feingold, combined the results of thirty studies which looked at the stereotype we hold in the West of the physically attractive. Compared to less attractive people, the more attractive were seen as 'more sociable, dominant, sexually warm, mentally healthy, intelligent, and socially skilled'. (They were not, however, rated higher on one cluster of character traits: 'honesty, genuineness, sincerity, trustworthiness, morality, kindness', which is something.)

In these studies, ratings were usually made of people in photographs. Obviously, as you get to know someone, over time their true personality reveals itself. But at the first encounter, physical appearance is one of the only pieces of information we have to go on, and human beings make very fast and not entirely conscious judgements at this point.

Is the stereotype correct?

But how accurate are these first impressions? Feingold went on to combine the results of ninety-three studies which looked at whether physical attractiveness was associated with personality, social behaviour, cognitive ability and sexuality.

Attractiveness turned out, contrary to the stereotype, to bear *no* notable relation to intelligence or personality measures of sociability, dominance and general mental health. What it was related to were things you might expect in a person to whom everyone is automatically nice on sight, and whose acquaintance they wish to pursue. Good-looking people were 'less lonely, less socially anxious, more popular, more socially skilled, and more sexually experienced'.

Why do we make snap judgements?

Why is it that we keep on making so many (often incorrect) judgements on the basis of that first glance? We often leap to conclusions based on facial features, too: for example, strong jaw = strong character; thin lips = 'tight-lipped' = reticent. Psychologists think we do this in an attempt to make the world more orderly and predictable. When we meet someone for the first time, we feel the need to get a fast grip on what they're like so that we have an idea of how to deal with him or her.

For some characteristics, a self-fulfilling prophecy may be involved. Feingold suggests that one reason for the perpetuation of the 'good-looking' stereotype is that, because we are so responsive to good-lookers, the latter may be more responsive in return in those situations. But that doesn't mean they have corresponding *traits* of character, such as sociability. We tend to think that other people's behaviour stems from their personality, while overlooking the effect of the situation they're in.

Again, if a man is huge with a gigantic jaw, people may defer to him and he might indeed become rather dominant. There is also some very recent evidence that, given photos of faces, panels of judges can predict people's warmth and dominance with some accuracy. It may be that our faces develop habitual expressions – and these certainly could reveal something about us.

But we are talking in generalizations here. What is clear is that for any *specific* individual, making judgements of any kind on sight is a highly risky business. We need to learn to 'hold' our first impressions in the absence of sufficient information, and to be nice to *everyone* on first meeting them . . .

SEXUAL ATTRACTION

There is a second problem. Let's return to you and your girlfriend at the party. You might both make certain general judgements about the man on the other side of the room; yet one of you fancies him to death and the other doesn't. So on top of judgements of physical attractiveness and character is the gut feeling of *sexual* attraction. Or, in the case of your girlfriend, that feeling is missing.

Lovemaps

The only plausible clue to this sexual tug that I have found is at this point only a theory, which has not been tested by experiment. The original idea was put forward by an American psychologist called John Money, who specializes in sexual deviations. He thinks that we each develop a unique subliminal guide to our ideal partner, what he calls a 'lovemap'. This guide consists of a list of cues which trigger feelings of sexual arousal in us – things like the shape of a mouth, a knobbly nose, big blue eyes, a particular walk or a deep, rumbling laugh. The more of our individual choice of cues a person has, the more likely we are to feel sexually attracted to them.

But what determines what those cues will be? Money implies that they will be things that have been linked in the past with feelings of sexual arousal. So, for example, if we were once particularly sexually excited and happened to catch sight of a fireman through the window, ever afterwards we may be sexually aroused by firemens' uniforms. Money also thinks that our lovemaps are built up in childhood and pretty well set in stone by the time we are adolescents.

It is certainly plausible that we have learned to associate certain cues with sexual arousal. However, I believe that is too limited a view. I think it is very probable that we also learn to associate certain cues with feelings of being loved and cared for. So, for example, if you have a father who loves you very much and who has a particular laugh, it may be that when you hear a very similar laugh you recall warm feelings of love and security. That memory may not be particularly conscious; it could well be subliminal – beyond your awareness – and yet still able to have an effect. So we know that we feel happy at the sight of someone, but we don't know why.

Indeed, the British psychiatrist John Bancroft has suggested to me that some people may choose a partner who looks like one of their parents or, interestingly, like themselves. This is because such a partner creates a sense of familiarity or security. For these people, familiarity and security makes it easier to become sexually aroused. (For others, unfamiliarity and the 'dangers' of insecurity might be more sexually stimulating.)

There's another problem with Money's concept. I do not believe that the maps are fixed when we are still young. I think that they can change and develop and be added to throughout life. If, say, you have a raging passionate affair in your fifties with a man who has bushy eyebrows, bushy eyebrows may well make their way into your map.

Money does not say what determines which features will end up in your map. Why might it be the bushy eyebrows and not, say, his hairline? Most likely, it will be the most memorable or idiosyncratic features of the person. It therefore seems reasonable to conclude that we might have several of each feature in our personal maps – several pairs of eyes, nose shapes, hair colours and so on.

Lovekits

Indeed, the word 'lovemap' seems inadequate – too rigid. Rather like the 'identikits' used by the police to compose faces, with choices of eyes, noses, mouths and other features, the word 'lovekits' may be a better description. What we have here is a selection of cues, with perhaps several alternatives for each type, that we add to – and maybe subtract from – throughout life. If a person possesses enough of the cues which, for us personally, trigger feelings of sexual arousal – and maybe love and security too – then we are overcome with hot lusty flushes.

So what is happening at that party? What has that man got for you?

Ginger hair

Your first lover had hair just that shade. He was kind and funny and you had a great time, even though it didn't work out in the end.

Rocket-shaped nose

Your father, who loves you dearly – and whom you love – has a nose that could blast to the moon.

Bandy legs

At school you had the most almighty crush on the head boy. You often used to get a fine view of his muscly bandy legs as he powered down the rugby field.

Ears like dinghy sails

At a conference in Spain you had a passionate encounter with a man whose ears could have guaranteed victory in any yacht race.

Your girlfriend, in contrast, has no such associations – or perhaps one or two, but not enough to weaken her knees.

So at the very beginning of a potential relationship lies a great yawning pit. We are not only overcome with lust for someone who may or may not be a suitable lover, but we have made all sorts of character judgements that may or may not be true. Some will be judgements that your girlfriend might make too; others may be a result of your personal subliminal associations. If this man does subconsciously remind you of other people from your past, you might attribute some of their personality traits to him as well.

Physical attractiveness matching

Let's assume now that he has caught sight of you, and that your dark hair, green eyes, slightly lopsided smile and stocky legs have pressed his psychological buttons. He also may have been rather more affected than you are by your general level of physical attractiveness. Plenty of research has shown that, when choosing whom to date, physical attractiveness is more important to men than to women (highly irritating for us, of course).

However, the evidence is that, on the whole, people tend to be with a partner of roughly the same level of physical attractiveness as themselves (unless, of course, a significantly less attractive partner has something heavy to compensate such as money and power . . .). This is probably because we all want the most attractive person we think we can get, but if we aren't very attractive (or think we aren't) we won't aim too high and risk rejection. So we end up with someone at about our own level.

SIMILARITY

Let's take it you've pressed his 'buttons' and are in roughly the right attractiveness range, so that he thinks you won't laugh mockingly at any approach he makes. Let's assume that one of you has contrived to start a conversation, and that the initial signs are favourable. You can find things to talk about, and a rapid survey of the basics reveals that he isn't noticeably denser than you, thirty years older than he looks or just out of prison for computer fraud.

The fact is that we do tend to pair up with people roughly similar to ourselves in terms of age, intelligence, interests, education and social background. Obviously there are exceptions, but any wide disparities – in age, for instance – are risk factors for relationship break-up. A much older partner may well have quite different interests and values and ways of looking at the world, and these can spell trouble.

In the early stages of a relationship, women may be more alert to the importance of finding a similar partner than men are. Combining the results of a number of experiments, Alan Feingold has found that women value similarity in a partner more than men do. Given that similarity is an important contributory factor to the survival of a relationship, placing great weight on it is a wise strategy.

Feingold points out that these were rather artificial experiments, and we still need to see if the results are generally true in the real world. What we would expect to find, he says, is that the two sexes conduct themselves differently at social gatherings. 'Arriving men may quickly scan the room for the best-looking women [or, as I've said, the best-looking women they think they can get] and then focus all attention on those few women.' What's more, if the men are less concerned about similarity but are aware of its importance to women, they might try to persuade the selected women that they *are* similar to them.

Women, in contrast, might 'cast an initially wider net' than men, and be more likely to try to find out about prospective partners' attitudes and interests so as to weed out the inappropriate ones. And, interestingly, 'Women should be less likely than men to misrepresent themselves to the opposite sex because dissembling would be inimical to their objective of finding a similar partner.'

Active distortion

So there's something to watch out for – the possibility that after he's agreed fervently that gerbil breeding is the only hobby for a person of taste, he hares to the local pet shop to buy up a job lot (while privately thinking that, if the relationship doesn't prosper, gerbil stew might be interesting).

There's always a risk of some active distortion at the outset. And while women may be less likely to misrepresent themselves, there's no doubt that women sometimes buy football rattles and grit their teeth through hours of excruciating boredom, having assured the new boyfriend that they really can't think of a nicer way to spend a Saturday afternoon.

The distortion can also continue for some considerable time. One study, for instance, found that, even after twenty-one months, around a fifth of their sample were still avoiding topics that might reveal how different they and their partner really were, and were not disclosing things about themselves that they feared might damage their image in the other person's eyes.

SELF-DECEPTION

As well as active distortion, we're also perfectly capable of a lot of self-deception. The trouble is that, once we've got our theories about the other person up and running – which we can do frighteningly quickly – we tend to look for supporting evidence. More seriously, we ignore evidence that contradicts our beliefs about the potential partner. So if, for instance, we think the man has a similar sense of humour, we notice when he laughs – although we may not notice when he fails to laugh at something we find funny.

We may refuse to see his faults clearly, too. For example:

– You're both at a dinner party. You accept seconds of the delicious chocolate cheesecake. He says, laughing, 'She eats like she's trying for the *Guinness Book of Records.*' Everyone laughs dutifully.

   You think: 'What a wit he is!'

   Or: 'He's just being funny, he doesn't *mean* it.'

   If you were less besotted, you might think: 'I don't think it's nice to put me down in public/humiliate me for cheap laughs/taunt me about eating.'
– His sister's birthday is coming up. He has had a disagreement with her, and feels very much that he is in the right.

She has invited you both to her birthday party – clearly a peace offering. You think you should both go so that he and she can make up. He consistently refuses.

Besotted interpretation: 'He's a man of such strong principles. Full of integrity. Once he's made up his mind what's right, there's no moving him.'

Possible less besotted interpretation: 'Stubborn idiot.'

I must emphasize strongly here that I'm not suggesting you wait until a perfect, fault-free man comes along. You'd be waiting till the sun goes nova. The point is that it is vital to see clearly what his faults actually are. One of the problems that arise from the great washes of emotion in the very early stages of a relationship is that we don't want to see.

Warning signs

So we gloss over warning signs of faults in – or aspects of – the other person that we aren't going to be prepared to tolerate long-term. We might not want to tolerate them because:

1 Our personal make-up means that we have a low tolerance level for e.g. stubbornness/lack of humour/lack of consideration, and/or
2 His good qualities are not, for us, sufficient to outweigh his faults.

There are other warning signs that we might refuse to see – ones that indicate he may not be as over the moon about us as we are about him. For example:

– He says he'll phone tomorrow and doesn't. He says, 'So sorry, I was terribly busy. Crisis with the Hong Kong branch.' You choose to believe him. You squash the nagging thought that, if he was wild about you, a thirty-second call to tell you he'd got a crisis and couldn't talk, but arranging another time to ring, wouldn't have killed him.

If that happens once or twice, you need to say something. Don't use accusatory tones – the 'you inconsiderate jerk' approach – but just say how you feel. 'When you don't ring on the day you say you will, I feel a bit upset. Obviously I realize you have some desperately busy days. I'd just really appreciate it if you rang for ten seconds to tell me that was what was happening, and I *promise* I won't keep you talking.'

It is perfectly possible for a man to behave like this and genuinely not realize how he is upsetting you. He just assumes: 'She'll understand. Can't be helped. I'll ring tomorrow.' He also may think that he can't make a phone call that only lasts ten seconds, because *that* might upset you. So it is only fair to let him know how you feel.

The issue then becomes – does he keep on doing it? If he does, this is something you need to consider carefully. It may be that he isn't as crazy about you as you'd like him to be, or that he doesn't listen to and show concern for your feelings. Either way, it's a warning sign. And here's another:

– He makes remarks along the lines of:
  'Marriage? It's for sissies.'
  'I'm planning to go round the world next year.'
  'Jane's moved in with Michael, you know? The fool, she's nailed his feet to the floor now.'

Such comments reveal something about his attitude to commitment. Don't ignore them.

But there's no need necessarily to panic either. There's evidence that, even in couples who eventually marry, at any particular moment the man and the woman can have different levels of commitment to each other and to the idea of this being a long-term relationship. So even if he isn't as committed as you would like him to be, this doesn't mean he won't become so. The trouble is, it's also perfectly possible that he won't.

The main thing is that it's important to *notice* warning signs. They may vanish over time, you may conclude that what they are warning you of is true but you don't mind terribly – or you may decide that they point to something significant and worrying.

How to tell?

It is sometimes hard to work out whether something *is* actually a warning sign or not. Probably the best way to tell is to ask yourself a few questions:

1 Am I feeling uneasy?
2 What *exactly*, if I think about it closely, am I feeling uneasy about? Is it some particular thing that he has done or said? Or is it something that he has *not* done or said?
3 What do I think it might mean?
4 Is there any other evidence that supports my theory – or theories – about what it might mean? One crucial clue is: has that particular piece of behaviour – or actions on the same lines – been repeated on a number of occasions?

Feelings of unease should never be ignored. The trouble is that they often are, because we fear the consequences of following that particular train of thought. However, the brutal truth is that it is better to do that than to continue ruthlessly to suppress them. Otherwise the problem (if there is one) will not be faced, and the blindingly clear insight into your partner or your relationship will come two days after you've christened the baby.

Worrying answers

Let's look at some sample answers to those four questions.

1 Yes, I'm feeling uneasy.

2 Not sure why, exactly. Well ... I was a bit worried when he saw his ex-girlfriend for lunch last week, and he was a bit off with me all that evening.

3 I thought maybe he'd had a bad day at work or something. Or maybe he was unhappy to see her because it reminded him of a failed relationship. But I'm really afraid that he's realized he still loves her, and even though she's got someone else now, he now knows that in comparison he doesn't love me.

4 OK, I do have several theories. Any evidence?

a Had a bad day at work? Could be, but he's had bad days at work at other times and not been off with me.

b Unhappy because he was reminded of a failed relationship? And he doesn't want to be hurt again? Could be. Don't know.

c He's remembered what love is now he's seen her again? And his feelings for me don't match up? Could be. It was she who finished their relationship, after all – not him. Actually, I have to say that he has been not himself with me several times since then. Less overtly affectionate, even snapped at me once or twice. But it could still be theories (b) or (c).

So it looks as though the best thing would be to ask him, in a calm, non-threatening way: 'I feel you've not been quite yourself since you saw Janey. If it's made you feel differently about me in some way, I'd really much rather you told me straight.'

He may refuse to tell you. But if your uneasy feelings persist – because his slightly odd behaviour does – you will need to ask the question again. A man who persistently refuses to tell you what is wrong when you have a very strong sense that something *is* wrong might actually have a communication problem. If so, that could give you a lot of trouble if you did commit yourself to him, and it might be worth giving this some very serious thought.

But it is very important to say here that you can have uneasy feelings which are *not* grounded in reality. They can arise because it's a new relationship and you feel very uncertain about how it's going. If so, don't feel that you're being unusually over-anxious. Many people feel uncertain on this question for quite a long time.

Uneasy feelings can also arise because you have low self-esteem. You don't feel you're much of a catch – so why the hell would he want to be with you anyway?

Low self-esteem can be a killer, and I shall have a great deal more to say about the subject later. But for now, let me say that people with low self-esteem usually underplay their good qualities; they either don't see how many they have, or underestimate the importance of those that they do acknowledge. This man has *chosen* to date you, and will not be horse-whipped if he doesn't. So you're not perfect; nor is he, remember. (Though if you're in the first flushes of love, this can be hard to believe, of course.)

Reassuring answers

So let's run through those four questions again.

1 Yes, I'm feeling uneasy.
2 Not sure why, exactly. Well ... I was a bit worried when he saw his ex-girlfriend for lunch last week, and he was a bit off with me all that evening.
3 I thought maybe he'd had a bad day at work or something. Or maybe he was unhappy to see her because it reminded him of a failed relationship. But I'm really afraid that he's realized he still loves her, and even though she's got someone else now, he now knows that in comparison he doesn't love me.
4 Corroborating evidence. Well, when I come to think about it, actually he's been perfectly loving and normal since then. Maybe he *had* just coincidentally had a bad day at

work. In fact, now I remember, he did say something about Jenkins in Accounts being difficult.

Action: none.

Pursue those uneasy feelings

Running through these two examples of trains of thought illustrates two very important points. When you want to examine uneasy feelings:

- Make sure you think of as many alternative explanations as possible before looking for evidence for and against each one. Don't just pick the worst possible one and cling on to it, panicking.
- Don't pick on one particular action and generalize it without thought. If the other person has a rare evening when he doesn't behave quite as normal with you, set that against the vast majority of evenings when he's loving to you. In other words, look at the whole wall, not at one or two bricks.

  The time to worry is if those evenings increase in frequency.

So don't let those uneasy feelings lie. Pursue them, even if they turn out to be based on your anxieties rather than on what's really happening. (But pursue them in your thoughts before deciding whether or not to take action; if you start anxiously questioning him every five minutes you'll drive him potty.) The biggest potential for trouble comes when you refuse to notice them. By the time their true meaning becomes clear, you may have devoted considerable time and emotional energy to something that isn't going to provide what you want, and might cause you a great deal of pain when it ends.

MOTIVES – YOURS AND HIS

When you're swimming happily about in the emotional pools
of the early stages of a relationship, you can sometimes fail
to see that your motives for being in the relationship may
not be the same as his.

The fact that he is very sexually passionate towards you,
for instance, can sometimes be misinterpreted. The evidence
is that men are, in general, more likely to separate sex and
emotion than women are. Obviously a man's sexual passion
can reflect his love for you, and women can have sex without
emotional attachment – we're only talking in generalities
here. But it points to a potential danger – that the intensity
of a man's sexual passion is taken to be more psychologically
significant than it actually is.

Passion is just one extremely strong motive for being in a
relationship. So are:

- desire for pleasant companionship
- feelings of loneliness
- all your friends have got someone except you
- wanting the 'status symbol' of having a nice partner to
  show off
- wanting a confidant(e)
- wanting to blot out the pain of the break-up of a previous
  relationship
- needing to boost your self-esteem
- wanting someone to love
- wanting to be loved
- seeking a potential long-term commitment

You and your new man may each have a selection of these
motives. They may not overlap, and they may not always
bode well for his long-term intentions.

This may not matter at all, if you are happy just to enjoy
the relationship for its own sake. You may be very relaxed

about doing exactly this, and if it turns into something more serious, fine; if not, you've had fun anyway. What I *am* concerned about is someone who is on the look-out for a permanent partner, and who is therefore going to be made far more unhappy about the relationship not working out.

It may be hard to discern what the other person's motives are (sometimes, even, what your own motives are). It's important not to assume that, because this new person is entering into a relationship with you, he too is in search of a major commitment. He may well not be. He may, indeed, not even regard your relationship as a 'relationship' at the beginning. He may see it as casual dating, and be alarmed or feel pressured if he discovers you have already given it a more serious (in his eyes) label. He could still be seeing other women, which you may not realize. So, given that you both fit each other's lovekits and are feeling rather excited, it's wise not to let this situation trigger a whole set of assumptions about the other person's feelings for you and a possible future together.

At this point in the game, all you know is that you find each other sexually attractive and you're generating enough electricity to power the *QE2*. You will quickly get some very broad idea about his character – whether he an extravert or an introvert, warm or cool in his dealings with others, and so on – and some basic biographical details: age, education, current job. You may, indeed, rapidly conclude that you are in love. But are you?

ARE YOU IN LOVE?

In one sense, of course, you are if you say you are. And whether you 'really' are or not might not matter if it wasn't for the fact that, in the West at least, we seem to have endowed the concept with almost magical powers. We think that once two people say they love each other, love is such a powerful bonding agent that they can breathe a huge sigh of relief and relax. Hand in hand, they saunter off into the sunset.

The myths of romance

I blame the vast amount of romantic fiction to which we are all exposed. And if you think we women have been pretty heavily soaked in romantic myths, pity the men. Astonishingly, one study, by American psychologists Patricia Frazier and Ellen Esterly, found that men hold certain romantic beliefs more strongly than women. For example: 'Romantic love often comes only once in a lifetime', 'Somewhere there is an ideal mate for most people', 'Love doesn't make sense; it just is', and 'Love at first sight is often the deepest and most enduring type of love'. A possible explanation is that men are more emotionally dependent on love relationships, because their relationships with women are more intimate than those with their male friends. Women are likely already to have several psychologically close and supportive relationships with female friends.

Reality, of course, is very different. Many people love more than once in their lives; different 'mates' may be 'ideal' in different respects; love may not always be easy to understand, but we can certainly have a reasonable stab at it. And as for 'love at first sight' – my view is that this is a label we give to that powerful first surge of sexual attraction, *if* it later leads to a long and happy relationship. So in retrospect, years later, you gaze fondly at each other and say, 'Well, it was love at first sight, wasn't it? There we were, at Dave's Mobile Disco, and . . .' Conveniently forgetting that you'd probably felt many other surges of sexual attraction in your time, which had come to nothing. In retrospect, those surges would be referred to in cooler terms. 'Oh, I fancied him briefly. It wore off after he spent the first two hours of our first date talking about his sick gearbox and hiccuping carburettor.' Or, if the relationship lasted quite a short time: 'I was absolutely infatuated with him, you know. Love? Oh no, no.' Or else you just forgot about it.

But you see the problem – if in our heart of hearts we hold very romantic beliefs about the power of love, we can end up in bad trouble. This can come about not just once the relationship is established – which I'll come to later – but at the very beginning if we assign that label to our feelings extremely fast. We will immediately feel that our entire destiny depends on how this relationship works out, the old rose-tinted spectacles get glued to our faces, our brains become totally disengaged and we just can't see a thing.

A theory of love

To muddy the waters still further, the word 'love' can have different meanings. One theory of love, put forward by American psychologist Robert Sternberg, is too recent for much relevant research to have been done on it. My justification for mentioning it here is that it illustrates how the term 'love' can be used in a variety of ways. Sternberg argues that we can view love as consisting of three elements:

- *passion*
- *intimacy* – understanding, sharing deeply personal ideas and feelings, receiving and giving support and affection
- *commitment* – in the short term, the decision that you love the other person; in the long term, feeling committed to maintaining that love

These three elements can be put together in eight combinations.

1 *Non-love.* No elements present.
2 *Liking.* Intimacy only. What you mean when you say you 'love' someone in a non-sexual way.
3 *Infatuated love.* Passion only. No intimacy or commitment at this point.
4 *Empty love.* Commitment only. The feeling you might have in a very stale long-term relationship, where the passion and intimacy have withered.

5 *Romantic love.* Passion + intimacy. But not yet the commitment.

6 *Companionate love.* Intimacy + commitment. What you might get in a long-term relationship where the passion has been pretty well extinguished.

7 *Fatuous love.* Passion + commitment. Highly dangerous – the whirlwind courtship scenario. Making the commitment in the absence of intimacy and a true knowledge of the other person.

8 *Consummate love.* Passion + intimacy + commitment. The full works, which is what most of us would like to have.

Whatever future research findings show about this theory, I believe the idea that love can be composed of various elements in different proportions in a particular relationship is a valid one. You can see how there may be danger early on – you may label your feelings 'love' in the absence of elements that are necessary to its survival. Intimacy and/or commitment may be missing. It is also clear that, if he clutches you to his bosom early on and says, 'I love you, darling,' he may not mean quite what you think he means. You find yourself gazing at diamond rings in jewellers' shops, while he is thinking solely about his next hot date with you.

At the beginning of a relationship, the awful truth is that you simply cannot go on the strength of your feelings – or the apparent strength of his – as signs that you have made a good choice. Only time is going to reveal that.

2

Courting

Now you've got over the very early stages. The phone calls are increasing. You're seeing each other more often.

BONDING

Courtship is a time of exploration, into the other person and into your – at this stage still unpredictable – relationship. We want to act in such a way as to make this exploration easier, and to feel a sense of movement (but without, if you're wise, rushing things). There are two ways in particular to achieve both the exploration and the movement.

Joint activities

Bonding well with another person is more than just a matter of sighing at each other over candle-lit restaurant tables. The evidence is that doing a wide range of activities with each other has a better prognosis than doing only a few. In one American study, by social psychologist Ellen Berscheid and her colleagues, students were given a list of thirty-eight diverse activities. They included:

- *fun*: e.g. 'went dancing', 'visited friends', 'went to a play'

- *leisure interests*: 'outdoor recreation, e.g. sailing', 'went to a museum/art show', 'attended a sporting event'
- *work*: 'attended class', 'worked on homework'
- *intimacy*: 'discussed things of a personal nature', 'engaged in sexual relations'
- *practical activities*: 'did laundry', 'prepared a meal', 'went to a grocery store'

The students had to tick which of the thirty-eight activities they had done alone with their boyfriend/girlfriend in the previous week. The findings showed that the greater the range of activities a couple did together, the more likely it was that their relationship was still intact nine months later. Doing a lot of different things together seemed a better predictor even than measures of reported feelings.

So binding ourselves together with joint activities is one way in which relationships progress: the gradual intertwining of your lives can make the other person seem increasingly important. The other great value of doing a variety of things together, in my view, is that it helps you to learn more about what he's really like – how he reacts in different circumstances, how similar your tastes are, how well you operate as a team. It might be vital, after all, to find out if he's the sort of person who wants to drag you to three separate supermarkets just to get the best deal on a frozen pepperoni pizza.

Increasing self-disclosure

For a relationship to develop, you need to build up trust between the two of you. To do that, according to psychologists John Holmes and John Rempel, you need to take risks – in particular, to make yourselves vulnerable to each other. This can be very frightening. Even when a person wants a relationship badly, fears may hold him or her back. Six fears in particular have been suggested by social psychologist Elaine Hatfield:

- fear of hurt and rejection
- fear of losing one's individuality or of being engulfed
- fear of having one's faults exposed
- fear of one's destructive impulses if one were to 'unleash' one's feelings
- fear that information disclosed now will later be used as ammunition
- fear of losing control

So for many of us it is alarming to move deeper into a relationship, since as you do so the other person gains increasing power over your life. Therefore, to say something that makes you vulnerable – for instance, something more loving than you've said before, or revealing some secret from your past which is perhaps not entirely creditable – is a major matter.

Ideally, you hope for a good response from your partner – leading you to trust him more – and you'll want reciprocity. If you say 'I love you,' you want him to say it back. And not just in an automatic, polite manner – if you always say it first, that won't feel right. But if there is reciprocity over time – sometimes you say it first, sometimes he does – then you'll feel reassured, and as though progress is being made.

By increasing your disclosure of your personal thoughts, feelings, past actions, beliefs and so on – and by him doing the same – you will feel there is movement in your relationship. It will also further the vital goal of finding out more about each other. But this needs to be a gradual process. Telling your entire life story to someone – including every grisly detail – right away is not the best move. It will feel inappropriate to the recipient, and that may put him off. And he is very unlikely to want to reciprocate.

So take it gently. At first, rather than revealing all in a Niagara Falls of confession, you're actually much more likely to want to present a terribly good image of yourself. This is natural. He, don't forget, will be busy doing that too.

But for the relationship to progress, the mask is gradually

going to have to slip. You're going to have to strip off the Proust jacket from the book by your bed, revealing the Jeffrey Archer beneath. You're going to have to admit that you cook like an arsonist. You're going to have to tell him about that time when you. ... No, I'm not suggesting that you have to inform him of every detail of your disgraceful past, but there may be things important to you which, in the end, you *should* feel you can tell him.

UNCERTAINTY

Let's assume your relationship is at least on the move. But whatever your own feelings, you may still be uncertain about his.

Secret tests

Have you ever done any of the following?

- Set up a situation where he's got to choose between your relationship and something else he really wants? Let's say he's angling for promotion and has been invited to sit at the 'top table' at his company's annual dinner. You 'inadvertently' organize a party to celebrate five years in your job on the very same evening, and argue that you will be terminally mortified if he fails to turn up.
- Started dropping the name of one of your colleagues frequently into the conversation. 'Kevin was brilliant with the managing director over the Kittyfood account'; 'Kevin was so kind, helping me with my report'; 'Kevin was wearing such a stunning new suit yesterday.' And have you watched your partner closely for any signs of green tinges, comments about what a stupid name Kevin is, questions about whether it's time you left this job for higher things?

   Kevin, unbeknownst to your man, is the office nerd who has spots, halitosis and no conversation.

- Told him that your aged Auntie Nellie has had a bit of a turn and you think you must spend the next six weekends with her. You checked his reaction. Upset but understanding? Understanding and indifferent? Oh *no* – trying not to look pleased?
- Tried to get his best friend to tell you what he really feels about you.
- At a party, you saw your man in conversation with an attractive woman. You watched with the vigilance of an air traffic controller. Was that an over-intimate smile? Did he touch her arm? Is he standing too close? Is he laughing a lot?
- Took him to a social event, presented him as 'my partner', and observed him closely. Did he go white? Did he look uncomfortable? Did he smile happily?
- Dropped hints about going on holiday together? Made jokes about men not being able to live alone without giving themselves salmonella poisoning and drowning in a sea of niffy socks?

According to American researchers Leslie Baxter and William Wilmot, many people (women more than men) do use such 'secret tests' to check out their partner's feelings. This may be because 'the state of the relationship', another of these researchers' studies found, is the top 'taboo topic' between romantic partners. Perhaps this is because we are afraid of being told something we don't want to hear; or because we see it is too soon and don't want to be seen as pressurizing.

Risks of secret tests

The trouble with secret rests is that
1 They might well damage the relationship. Trying emotional blackmail to see if he'll give up something he really values for you; the 'let's create a fictitious rival' tactic; the 'let's withdraw a bit from the relationship and see if he minds' strategy; putting his friends in embarrassing positions; all these are *not* brilliant ways of strengthening the still fragile bonds between you, and may do them active harm.

2 They may also be misleading. You and he may have different levels of commitment to the relationship at any one point in time, even if you both become equally committed to each other in the end. If he seems to be flirting with another woman at a party, this could mean he doesn't feel quite as enmeshed in your relationship as you do at this point. But it doesn't mean he won't become so. Indeed, it could also be that he always flirts with women – it's his style and doesn't mean anything (if this distresses you, it is something you can discuss with him further down the line). Or he might actually not be flirting with her at all – perhaps he's just enjoying a nice conversation, and would certainly not appreciate any accusations. Would you, every time you had a pleasant conversation with another man at a party? It would drive you mad.

Equally, a secret test of the 'hints and jokes' variety might be misleading. He may not feel that he's ready to commit to a holiday – never mind moving in with you – yet. But that doesn't mean he won't when he's ready.

I know it can be very tempting to apply secret tests, because evidence of commitment moves a relationship on and makes you feel it's developing. But if you can manage to restrain yourself and not try them out, you will probably be doing yourself and your budding relationship a big favour.

PATTERNS OF COURTSHIP

You will, however, very probably need to feel that your courtship *is* progressing. Evidence from studies by psychologists Ted Huston, Catherine Surra and colleagues is that, looking at courtships which end in marriage there are – broadly speaking – four main courtship patterns.

1 *Accelerated.* Moving swiftly to near certainty of marriage within five months, certainty by ten to fourteen months.

2 *Accelerated-arrested.* Rapid start, with the probability of marriage rising fast within two to three months. Then slowing until about fifteen months, and finally moving to certainty of marriage.

3 *Intermediate.* Moving smoothly to certainty at about twenty months; or a bit less smoothly to twenty-eight.

4 *Prolonged.* A slow and rocky progression with lots of ups and downs. Certainty at between forty and sixty-four months.

Obviously these are averages, not rigid pathways, but this research does show distinguishable patterns. Sometimes, too, there may be an initial cautiousness before a smooth ride (perhaps one of you is involved with someone else at the start, or has had a lot of prior relationships and feels tentative about the whole business). Occasionally, after a relatively smooth rise to a high level of commitment, there can be a few ups and downs before the final commitment.

What this shows is that there is no fixed route for a courtship to follow. If he hasn't proposed by month seven, there's no need to panic and start leaving copies of *Brides Monthly* in the bathroom. However, there's evidence that relationships are particularly prone to break down at around fifteen to eighteen months. This is most likely to be because by that point the couple themselves, and their friends and relatives, tend to feel that the couple should know by now if it is going to work or not, and that if there's going to be a commitment now's the time. (Possibly a bit premature, I believe – as we'll see later.) If there isn't a commitment, then they may think they should call it off before spending more time on a relationship that isn't going to be long-term.

'Accelerated' pathways

The two 'accelerated' pathways seem to fit this 'it's time to decide' concept. They probably involve two people who both feel ready for commitment. Partners with these patterns tend to withdraw more from their social networks into 'couple-dom', do more things together (both fun activities and domestic chores) and are more emotionally bonded.

The accelerated pathway may become arrested because the couple have hit opposition from family and friends. You might say: 'No, surely not?' But the truth is that other people's opinions often do matter. One study looked at 'turning points' in premarital relationships – that is, points where commitment levels shifted noticeably. The findings showed that one in five turning points were down to the influence of outsiders, and their influence was more likely to be negative than positive. Commitment was more likely to drop because social networks didn't approve than to rise because they did.

'Intermediate' pathway

The intermediate pathway may involve partners who aren't, in fact, absolutely sure about their compatibility. And/or one person may have a more positive attitude to marriage than the other, and applies pressure (of varying degrees of subtlety) to push the other person in the direction of the altar or registry office.

'Prolonged' pathway

The prolonged pathway is marked out from the others by the fact that there's noticeably more conflict between the partners. This is so despite the fact that they say they love each other just as much as couples who follow the other three pathways do.

None of the studies of courtship patterns went on to look at how happy the subsequent marriages were. But we do know that a lot of prolonged conflict is not a good sign. Of course there will be conflict in any relationship. But what matters is how it is dealt with (I shall have much to say on this later). If a couple keep up a high level of conflict, the signs are that they are not very good at dealing with it and resolving it. This could be very problematic in the long term.

None-love motives for marriage

Partners in a prolonged courtship may still end up marrying because they do feel they love each other; and there can be a lot of motives for marrying other than love.

- you've been in this relationship for several years and you don't want to feel you've made a dreadful mistake all this time. You've invested a lot in it; and you may even have some quite serious commitments already, such as having bought a house together
- your parents are nagging you
- one or other of you wants a child
- everyone in your circle is married but you
- you reckon you might not find anyone better
- You fear no one else will ever love you

I am sure you can think of a few more.

But it doesn't take a genius to see that these are all poor reasons for getting married. Or, if you don't want to get married, making some extremely serious commitment such as having a child together.

RELUCTANCE TO COMMIT

The truth is that, if your courtship seems to be going on an unconscionably long time with no committing moves from the other person, even though you yourself feel he is the right partner for you (and you don't have/have worked through any uneasy feelings, as discussed in Chapter 1), it really is important to try to find out why. You don't want to inveigle the other person into marrying you for any of the unfortunate motives listed above. You're not going to be thrilled if the happiest-looking person at your wedding is the bridegroom's mother.

So you need to ask yourself some very difficult questions.

1 Is he not quite sure you're the right person for him long-term?
2 Are you falling out a lot and regularly, which often makes the relationship uncomfortable?
3 Is he against serious commitment for some reason? And/or even though you love him, are you yourself worried about the whole idea of commitment?

Is he not quite sure you're the right person for him long-term?

Assuming you have been together for some time, you need to know what it is he's not quite sure about, and whether what it is is changeable, and whether you *do* in any case want to change it.

For instance, he may be hesitating because the truth is that he'd like a bit more of a domesticated partner – someone whose work was rather less important to her than it is. Someone who had rather fewer friends and a less active social life.

So how can you find out whether this is the truth or not? Usually, he will have dropped clues. These may have not been very obvious, and you may either not have noticed or have dismissed their importance, particularly if he's said them in a joking manner. 'Oh,' – to brand-new acquaintances – 'she's got more friends than I've had hot dinners!'

Once you've alerted yourself to these kinds of comments, you can work out whether they form a rather persistent theme and source of running jokes at dinner parties. It is, of course, perfectly possible for your tendency to reduce casseroles to charred embers to be a running joke and yet not a problem for him. If it is a problem, you may detect a certain steely undertone to his voice or that his laugh doesn't quite reach his eyes.

In an ideal world, of course, he would tell you straight what the matter is. But the world of relationships is far from ideal. He may not want to say anything to hurt you or rock the boat; he may not indeed be fully conscious of what his feelings really are. All he knows is that he's just not quite ready for commitment yet.

If you decide that he is hesitating because he's not convinced of your compatibility, and you have one or two theories about this, you may have to be very brave and ask him. This is, of course, potentially dangerous talk. It may even feel rather awkward and embarrassing, if you suspect that sexual difficulties might be a core problem.

Assuming you do get the truth out of him, it may be that he would really like you to be different in certain ways; or the relationship to be different somehow.

You would then need to ask yourself if these are changes you *can* make; and if you can make them, whether or not you *want* to. Going back to the example of him wanting a more domesticated, less work-oriented partner – could you change that? And, frankly, *would you want to*?

It would be natural for the whole idea of serious relationship talk like this to bring you out in a cold sweat. But after a long enough time, it really is better to face it than to let things drag on another five years.

Are you falling out a lot and regularly, which often makes the relationship uncomfortable?

If you are, it's a serious matter. There is no evidence that a good screaming match 'clears the air'. Rather, a mark of unhappy relationships is that the couple get into frequent negative cycles of attack and counter-attack. If you can't manage to deal with conflict successfully before the wedding, there's no reason to think you're going to get any better at it afterwards.

Some couples fall out to the extent that they break up and then get back together. More than once, I fear, is not a good sign. One study compared couples who were divorced with those who were still married. All the couples had had at least one premarital break-up. The results showed that 50 per cent of the divorced couples had split up two or three times during their courtship; but only 29 per cent of the couples who were still together had done so.

So if your front door is nearly off its hinges with over-slamming, think carefully. . . .

Is he against serious commitment for some reason? And/or even though you love him, are you yourself worried about the whole idea of commitment?

This can be a tricky one. There is evidence that both women's and men's attitudes to love tend to fall into one of three main patterns. Which of these three descriptions, written by American psychologists Cindy Hazan and Phillip Shaver, best fits you?

1 'I find it relatively easy to get close to others and am comfortable depending on them. I don't often worry about being abandoned or about someone getting too close to me.'
2 'I find that others are reluctant to get as close as I would like. I often worry that my partner doesn't love me or won't want to stay with me. I want to get very close to my partner, and this sometimes scares people away.'
3 'I am somewhat uncomfortable being close to others; I find it difficult to trust them completely, difficult to allow myself to depend on them. I am nervous when anyone gets too close, and love partners often want me to be more intimate than I feel comfortable being.'

Which of these three descriptions do you think best fits your partner?

Obviously these three patterns are not rigid boxes, but they do seem to be broad tendencies that researchers have found to be distinguishable. The patterns are labelled as follows:

1 *Secure*: you find it easy to get close to others and to trust them.
2 *Anxious*: you become obsessively preoccupied with a partner, and worry a lot that he doesn't love you.
3 *Avoidant*: you are uncomfortable with intimacy and closeness.

The same three patterns have been found in infants' relationships with their mothers. (The research was done on mothers, but the findings can almost certainly be extended to cover the main carer or carers of the child.)

Children who are 'securely attached' have mothers who are consistently sensitive and responsive to them.

Children who are 'anxious/ambivalent' have mothers who respond to them inconsistently. They are sometimes neglectful and unresponsive, and at other times intrusive. So the child becomes extremely preoccupied with the mother's availability and feelings towards him or her.

Children who are 'avoidant' have mothers who are rejecting. When they need comfort, they do anything but run to mother.

Cindy Hazan and Phillip Shaver, were the first to test if the three patterns which had been found in children could also be found in adult romantic partnerships. And their research found that indeed they can.

The two may be linked. Obviously memory can be deceiving, but there's evidence of at least some connection between relationships with adult partners and the ones people remember having with their parents when they were children. The theory is that when we are tiny, we start to build up in our heads models of what relationships are like – and how deserving we are of love.

If we are secure, we believe that other people are to be trusted, and that we are worthy of love. So we feel comfortable with close relationships.

If we are anxious, we want love but don't feel that loved figures are to be relied upon. So we are vigilant in relationships and worry about whether we are loved.

If we are avoidant, we feel others are not to be trusted, and that we don't deserve to be loved anyway. So we want to keep a distance in our romantic relationships.

But obviously, although you'd expect your experiences with your parents to be very important, people are complex and can react in different ways to these experiences. What's more, they are certainly not the only relationships we have in life! It's vital to emphasize here that, whatever mental working models we develop as children (which may be influenced by people other than our parents, too), they are not set in stone. Hazan and Shaver have pointed out that they can be influenced by relationships we have in later life, and that we can also shift our mental models through insight into them. You can't begin to alter your view of things and your actions without being aware of what you *are* doing. Once you admit that you take one look at a potential relationship and scream like a banshee, you can start thinking about whether this response is strictly necessary.

Attachment style and experience of relationships

How is your experience of relationships affected by your own attachment style? Remember Robert Sternberg's three components of love? Two Israeli psychologists, Mario Mikulincer and Irit Erev, gave questionnaires to over three hundred students. They wanted to know how people with each of the three attachment styles regard those three components, which they defined as:

- *intimacy*: 'trust, affection, self-disclosure, supportiveness, caring, and understanding'
- *passion*: 'desire for union, attraction, dependence, and idealization'

- *commitment*: 'the decision to love and to preserve the relationship'

When the two researchers looked at those who had been in a heterosexual relationship for over a year and asked about respondents' love for their partners, the secure ones felt more intimacy than the avoidant and ambivalent; equal passion; and more commitment than the ambivalent.

But the researchers also asked how the respondents wished to feel about an *ideal* partner. Now it emerged that the ambivalent wanted to feel as much intimacy, passion and commitment as the secure (which, with the exception of passion, they were clearly *not* feeling).

The avoidant, it turns out, wanted both less intimacy and less passion than the other two groups. And, although they said they felt as committed as the secure did in their current relationship, in an *ideal* partnership they would like to be significantly less committed than the secure would.

But what did their partners feel about the respondents? Quite a few partners agreed to participate in the study. Partners of all three groups felt equally passionate; but partners of the secure and avoidant felt more intimate and committed than did the ambivalents' partners. The avoidant respondents, however, didn't realize this – they saw less intimacy and commitment in their partners than the partners actually felt.

The secure, then, seemed to be doing fine. They tended to be in relationships that correspond to what they wanted out of relationships.

The avoidant were in relationships where they felt less intimate than their partners did. 'Maybe these relationships will work out well in the long run,' the researchers say, 'gradually convincing avoidant people to become less avoidant, or perhaps the partners will eventually get fed up with loving and not being loved equally in return.'

The ambivalent were somehow not managing to set up the relationships that they would ideally like to have.

Whether this was due to deficient social skills, inner conflicts or the behaviour of partners is not known.

Crucially, there were no sex differences in any of these findings. What's more, 57 per cent of the participants classified themselves as secure, 28 per cent as avoidant and 15 per cent as ambivalent; and the proportions were similar for men and women. There is thus no evidence here, as all the media hype suggests, that men are more concerned with avoiding commitment than are women.

Matching of attachment styles

What sort of partner are you likely to choose, depending on your own 'attachment style'? Another study, by American psychologists Lee Kirkpatrick and Keith Davis, looked at over three hundred couples in serious dating relationships.

Surprisingly, the researchers found no avoidant-avoidant or anxious-anxious pairs. (This seems a shame in a way, because they would at least have known where the other person was coming from!)

Rather, nearly half the anxious women were with an avoidant man. In other words, they were in exactly the situation they most feared. Perhaps they felt comfortable with this – it was, after all, only what they expected.

Most of the avoidant women had a secure partner. Their relationships were, however, particularly likely to hit the dust later. (And avoidant and anxious people of either sex were less likely than the secure to be in a steady relationship in the first place.)

Three-quarters of the secure women chose a secure man; the rest were evenly split between the two insecure types. This sounds potentially problematic – but might an insecure person change? There's some recent evidence, the researchers point out, that around one person in four alters their attachment style in adulthood, mainly becoming more secure. So that's encouraging. Any banshee-like screaming or serious panic attacks at the sight of a relationship *can* be soothed.

The implications of his attachment style

If he is secure and yet not committing to you, the problem is unlikely to lie with his own attitude to commitment. It may lie with his fears about incompatibility or the difficulty you have as a couple in dealing with conflict. Or, indeed, it may have some other source, which you may only be able to discover by straightforward (but not aggressive!) questioning.

If he is anxious/ambivalent and not committing to you, it is unlikely to be because he just doesn't want commitment at any price. It may be for similar reasons to those which hold a secure man back – and he may also, at some deep level, fear that you don't really love him and will leave him some day.

If he is avoidant and not committing to you, as you will by now understand, this is par for the course. The fact that he is avoidant may even be obvious from his description of his relationship history. If it involves relationships with vast numbers of women, then the most likely explanation, in my view, is that he is avoidant.

His difficulties with commitment are nothing to do with you. He may, indeed, eventually bring himself to commit, but as the research I've described shows, he may not be totally comfortable with it.

The risk here is that women often believe *they* will be the one for whom a previously wayward man realizes the error of his ways. Very often, they are wrong. However, it does appear that some people can change from being insecure to being secure. Maybe your fantasy that you'll be the one to change him *will* come true!

What you probably have to decide is how much time and effort you're prepared to allocate to this project. Ideally, if inability to commit has been a serious problem with him all his life – and *if he sees it as a problem*, which he may not – he might be willing to seek some professional therapeutic help.

If he isn't willing to do *something* about it, then I think it's as well to be aware that, though you might win out here, there is also a strong chance that you won't. Therefore you need to decide on the length and depth of your investment, and try to discuss it with him too.

Many women will simply get fed up with an avoidant partner's commitment problems and leave him. There is, as you can tell – and this is the case with all love problems – no rule here. But to have an understanding of what might be going on in his head is, in my view, a better basis for decision-making than floundering around without a clue.

The research on attachment styles reinforces yet again the importance of realizing that, when someone says they love you, their whole approach to love might be different from yours. This area is one where tripwires can lie in wait for the incautious.

The implications of your attachment style

If you are secure, the chances are that you will have chosen a secure partner, and neither of you will have problems with commitment as such. Therefore if either of you is reluctant to commit after a long courtship, the reason must lie elsewhere. Rather than letting things drift on, it's better to explore what that reason – or reasons – might be.

If you are anxious/ambivalent, then you risk harming your relationship. This attachment style does women harm if they drive men away by being desperately anxious, jealous and possessive. The evidence is that possessiveness *is* one of the factors that can damage men's satisfaction with a relationship.

It is also the case that you might be particularly likely to choose an avoidant man, thus precipitating exactly the situation you most fear. There are two secrets to dealing with this one:

1 By gaining insight into what you are doing, you get the chance to change it. You can become wary of avoidant men, and look for more secure ones.

2 You make great efforts to alter your behaviour towards your partner. He's half an hour late picking you up, and you stop yourself spitting, 'I bet you took that blonde bimbo from reception out for a drink, didn't you?' He wants to spend two nights a week with his male friends. You refrain from going into a major sulk.

Our behaviour is alterable once we become aware of it. You won't be able to manage a radical change immediately. But with luck, you will be reinforced for any changes which you make by having a more pleasant relationship and more loving closeness with your partner.

'Darling, of course you must see the boys. I'll miss you, of course, but my gang have a lot of serious gossip and bottles of wine to get through too.'

'Thanks, sweetheart – and I'll miss you too.'

This attitude is better than unfair accusations and sulks, which will do your relationship no good at all.

If you find any change impossible to make, then you could consider seeking therapeutic help. Sometimes we can't get over the legacy of childhood and past experiences without some outside aid.

If you are avoidant, this can cause trouble too. Our attitude to love could do us harm if we constantly run away from or destroy relationships that might, if allowed to flourish, enhance our lives no end. And if you keep running away from relationships, you may also be less likely to pick up the sort of relationship skills needed to keep them going.

You may be lucky enough to find a secure partner, but as we've seen, these relationships are particularly likely to break up. There is evidence that women typically (but not always, of course) put more maintenance work into relationships than men do. So, Kirkpatrick and Davis argue, if you're not very motivated, or not sufficiently skilled, things may be especially likely to collapse because no one's working to keep the relationship going.

If, however, you try to give a relationship with a secure

man a real chance, this might help to alter your mental concepts of relationships. You might come to see that sometimes other people *can* be trusted, and that you are a lovable person. Again, if you feel you can't shift your ideas and yet you don't like them, you might consider getting some professional assistance.

THINGS TO WATCH OUT FOR

Ideally, people use the courtship period to suss out the other person and to discover how the two of them work together as a couple. After a while, a few of the scales slip from their eyes. Then, assuming neither of the pair is having problems with the idea of commitment as such, the issue becomes: well, is this It?

There are no perfect human beings. What we hope for is someone with the good qualities which we personally want and need, and faults which we can tolerate.

What you want and need

During the courtship period, we tend to be terribly concerned with what the other person thinks about us. I'm not sure that we always concentrate quite so intently on what we think about him. What do *we* want, and can he provide it?

Studies show that women would like a partner who is:

- kind
- considerate
- honest
- faithful
- reliable
- expressive (affectionate, compassionate, expresses tender feelings easily)
- possessed of a sense of humour
- ambitious and accomplished

Men like these qualities in a partner too, except that ambition is less important to them than it is to women (given that even nowadays women have less economic power than men, this discrepancy is hardly surprising). Physical attractiveness in a partner, as I mentioned earlier, is also more important to men than to women.

But these are qualities which most people would say they wanted. What is important is your *personal* list. You might, say, not be too bothered about his ambition. But you might want him to be very intelligent. Do you want him to be very outgoing and sociable, or rather quiet and introverted? Do you perhaps need someone who shares your profound political or religious views?

It might help to make lists of what you want and of his qualities, to focus your mind on what might suit *you*, rather than worrying about whether you fit his requirements. Two points here:

- Your dating partner might not have all the qualities you need. You then need to ask yourself – does he have the ones I *most* need?
- You can probably divide your list of his qualities into two columns: (a) characteristics which are unlikely to change radically (e.g. with the best will in the world, he won't be able to make himself cleverer). (b) ways of behaving which he could change if he wanted to, and which he might if he knew it was important to you (e.g. reliability, consideration).

I know this might sound dreadfully calculating, but I certainly don't mean it to be. What I do believe is that, before committing ourselves to a partner, we need to understand *ourselves* and our needs, as well as to have an understanding of the other person. Making lists, even if it's just in your head, is a way of focusing the mind. Otherwise you might just 'come to' not long after the wedding and discover that if you want a jolly night out, as you frequently do, you're not going to get much joy out of your new spouse. 'What, you want us to *go out*? Not on a Saturday. No way. I want a TV dinner and *Match of the Day*.'

What faults can you tolerate?

As with the 'what you want and need' list, this is going to consist of another idiosyncratic group of characteristics. There is, however, some evidence on partners' characteristics which are rather generally unpopular. In a study of couples who had been married no longer than a year, each partner was given a list of nearly 150 actions. They had to mark those things which their partner had done in the last year which had irritated, angered or upset them. What follows are those actions which they marked *and* which were linked with being less satisfied with their marriages, for both women and men. The researcher, American psychologist David Buss, calls these 'upset elicitors':

- being sexually withholding or rejecting
- moodiness
- over-possessiveness, jealousy and dependence
- being neglecting, rejecting and unreliable
- sexualizing others (e.g. talking about how attractive other women are)

Some upset elicitors were linked with dissatisfaction for women only (not because men would enjoy any of them, I'm sure; but probably because women are far less likely to act like this):

- acting condescending (e.g. 'placed more value on his opinions because he was a man', 'made me feel inferior')
- lack of consideration (e.g. 'left the toilet seat up', 'did not help clean up', 'burped or belched loudly', 'yelled at me', 'teased me about how long it took me to get dressed')
- drinking and smoking too much

- hiding all his emotions to 'act tough'
- sexual aggression

You could argue that, as they are just statistical links between the elicitors and being dissatisfied, perhaps it's being dissatisfied that causes the other person to behave in such a manner towards you. However, it is fair to say that the actions above are more characteristic of unhappy than of happy marriages, and at the very least are not going to help matters. The actions have, indeed, already been identified as upsetting or annoying. So it's likely that they can damage the marriage as well, perhaps, as being sometimes drawn out of the other person because *you* are unhappy.

Though this was a study of newly-weds, it has serious implications for the courtship phase. Quite a number of these sorts of behaviour (if not all of them) were probably already present at that stage, and ignored or down-played. It's not likely that they all sprang into being, fully formed, in the first year of marriage! So if your dating partner has faults of these kinds, think about it carefully.

Also bear in mind that this list of upsetting actions may get longer over time. In this study, within the first year few people had been unfaithful or abusive, which are extremely distressing situations to have to deal with. What's more, types of behaviour that you might be able to tolerate during courtship and early marriage might have a cumulative effect and become unbearable a few more years down the line.

One type of behaviour that is unbearable at *any* time is violence. A partner who is violent in marriage – an intolerable state of affairs – is quite likely to have been violent during courtship. So any signs of such behaviour must be taken extremely seriously. Don't make the mistake of saying to yourself, 'Oh, they'll be better when we're married.' Don't even contemplate marrying a man or woman who is violent to you *unless* they see they have a major problem and take themselves to a therapist. (I'll be discussing violence in more detail later.)

There are some general personality traits to watch out for, too. A couple of specific personality characteristics have been linked to a greater likelihood of divorce:

- neuroticism
- chronic ill-temper

Again, these are characteristics which, provided you can clear the fog from your rose-tinted glasses, will be visible before marriage. Or at least they should be.

Dangerous beliefs

There is another dimension to be considered. What ideas do you hold about relationships? A set of dangerous beliefs has been identified by two American psychologists, Roy Eidelson and Norman Epstein. Studies show that men and women who hold them are more likely to be unhappy with their relationship. They are:

1 That disagreement is destructive to relationships – making you less likely to face and resolve conflicts.
2 That mind-reading is expected – the idea that if someone loved you, they should be able to deduce what you want and need without you having to tell them (a very bad mistake).
3 That partners cannot change – so you feel there's little hope that problems can be solved.
4 That you have to be a perfect sexual partner – very inhibiting.
5 That the sexes are different – means that you look at your partner in a rather stereotyped way and this makes you less sensitive to his idiosyncratic desires and characteristics.

These five unrealistic beliefs tend to cluster together. So if you've got one, you've probably got the lot. They *must* be tackled, or you will risk hurting your relationship through things that are entirely in your own head. The truth is:

1 It would be impossible to have a relationship with another human being without there being conflict. It's not disagreement that's destructive to relationships, it's failing to tackle them properly (I'll be talking about conflict resolution in detail later).

2 It's vital to state your wants and feelings clearly. I cannot emphasize strongly enough that, no matter how much your man loves you, *he is not a telepath*. It's no good expecting him to make a huge fuss of your birthday, for instance, if (a) he never makes a fuss of his own and (b) he didn't know you wanted him to make a huge fuss. He'll just be utterly mystified as to why you've been so wretchedly sulky all day. He bought you a woolly jumper and a copper saucepan and you would have preferred jewels and flowers; he wondered if you'd like to go out for a pizza when you wanted a smart restaurant with linen tablecloths and respectful waiters.

3 There are many ways in which partners can change and problems in the relationship can be solved. It's no good flinging one's hands in the air in helpless despair at the first sign of trouble.

4 If you think you've got to be perfect in bed you'll just get yourself in a terrible state. You'll be rigid with tension and anxiety, and have to keep leaning over the side of the bed to consult complicated charts on the Congress of the Frozen Mushroom or whatever. You want to make him happy, not to display a vast array of techniques that would make a medieval Eastern concubine blush.

5 You can put a spanner in the works of understanding and communication with your partner by making the fact that he is A Man a terribly prominent part of your view of him. Sure he's a man, but he is primarily a unique human being. Stereotypes just get in the way of seeing a person clearly.

The end result of these beliefs may well be disappointment, disillusionment and feelings of 'growing apart'. But the thoughts we take into a serious relationship are something we can work on, and which we can talk about with a partner. Once we're focused on the dangers, we can start to fight them.

DON'T COMMIT TOO FAST

This brings me to the most important point I want to make about courtship. DON'T COMMIT YOURSELF TOO QUICKLY. As I've said, if courtships go on for several years with no hint of commitment or progress, then a few enquiries might be in order. But at the other end of the scale, it can take two or three years to get a reasonable idea of what the other person is like and how you fit together as a couple.

In one study of couples who had lived together before marriage (these figures are averages, of course):

− Those who were now *divorced* had:
    dated each other for 7.5 months
    then lived together for 14 months before marrying
    TOTAL: 21.5 months on average
− Those who were *still married* had:
    dated for about 20 months
    then lived together for 16 months before marrying
    TOTAL: 36 months on average

In another study, researchers found that the longer the courtship – up to two years, anyway – the more likely it was that a couple would stay together. (True, one hears of people who married after knowing each other for four weeks and are still happily together after fifty years. They've been extremely lucky, I'd say.)

Essentially, only time will bring you the information you need. What you want are:

1 A very good understanding of him. Time allows you to see his behaviour in a wide variety of circumstances: social, crisis, illness, the business of daily living. It will allow his characteristics gradually to be revealed.
2 An understanding of yourself.
3 A chance to evaluate how you work together as a couple. For instance:

Do you enjoy doing similar things?

Do you have similar tastes?

Do you have similar views?

Do you have similar ideas about what relationships should be like?

Do you have similar attitudes to having children?

Do you have fun together?

Can you resolve conflicts?

Can you talk to each other?

Can you reveal things to each other that might be humiliating, difficult or embarrassing?

Can you sort out practicalities – shopping, cooking, cleaning and so on – in a fairly equitable way?

I am not suggesting that you marry a clone of yourself – that would be boring. But the evidence is that we do want a partner's major attitudes and values to be like our own. Human beings seem to need validation from others that their view of the world is roughly correct. We need our partner above all to give us that validation.

Time is also needed for him, too. He has to understand and accept you as you are, he has to understand himself sufficiently to know how likely it is that you can both make it through in the long term, and he too has to evaluate how the relationship works day-to-day.

Many issues, as we have seen, need to be worked through during the courtship stage. Otherwise, you simply increase your chances of being a divorce statistic (or an 'oh no, single again' statistic). For many people, these issues are *not* resolved by the end of courtship. An American study, by psychologists Blaine Fowers and David Olson, found that signs of future trouble are already present in a large number of engaged couples.

Most of the couples in a nationwide sample were given a questionnaire by the member of the clergy who was to marry them, so of course are not entirely representative. The couples were mainly white and either Christian or, if not very religious, at least wanted to be married in a church. Nevertheless, the findings are salutary.

The 5030 couples turned out to be of four different types.

Vitalized: 28 per cent of these couples scored highly on nearly all the important relationship aspects which were measured. They were very happy with their partner's personality and habits; very comfortable with their ability to discuss feelings and resolve conflicts; satisfied with how they related in terms of affection and sex; happy with how they spent free time together and got on with each other's family and friends; they agreed on financial and parenting matters; they preferred egalitarian roles. However, they 'tended to be somewhat unrealistic in their expectations for marriage'.

Harmonious: 27 per cent had relationships of 'moderate' quality. Their scores were all right, but lower than those of the vitalized couples on most things. They were, like the vitalized couples, rather unrealistic about marriage, and 'had not come to a consensus on child-related issues such as the number of children they wish to have or their parental roles'.

Traditional: 23 per cent were moderately dissatisfied with all aspects of the relationship, yet stronger on forward planning. They tended to be realistic in their view of marriage and had agreed on the number of children they wanted and on their roles as parents.

Conflicted: 22 per cent had low scores in all areas. (It would be interesting to know why they were getting married.)

Nearly half of these engaged couples (conflicted and traditional), then, look to be in difficulty even before they've made it up the aisle; another quarter (harmonious) provide some grounds for worry. The 28 per cent 'vitalized' look most promising, but they have some unrealistic expectations and, since other evidence shows that marriages tend to decline in quality without good maintenance, a few of the vitalized ones may still come undone.

You need to see if you can sort out weak areas in your relationship *before* the Big Commitment. You don't want to be standing at the font holding your first-born and thinking, 'Oh *no*, what have I done?'

3

Communicating

We think talking is easy. The awful truth, however, is that talking *is* easy – but communicating isn't.

If you both now feel you're in this relationship for the long haul (you hope), communicating well – important at any time – becomes crucial. Failing to communicate properly can have serious consequences:

- It means you start to lose sight of how the other person is looking at the world, feeling and thinking.
- By losing sight in that way, you become increasingly unable to give the other person rewards that he needs. For instance, if you didn't know that he's having a crisis of confidence at work, you might not give him lots of praise and encouragement when he recounts to you his minor triumph over Wiggins in sales.
- You may fail to realize that he isn't happy with certain aspects of your relationship.

The same applies the other way round:

- He starts to lose sight of how *you're* looking at things.
- He doesn't realize what sort of rewards you need from him – the occasional romantic surprise, for instance.

– He won't know what worries you have about your relationship.

Most importantly, neither of you will be able to talk through problems and conflicts.

TECHNIQUES OF COMMUNICATION

There are certain specific mistakes that we often make when we talk to a partner.

Making what you say too general

Let's suppose that your partner is a hard worker, and quite often gets home late at unpredictable times. You are on tenterhooks not knowing when he's coming, whether to put the dinner on or not (as you're nearly always home first, perhaps, this seems to fall to your lot more often than not), whether to go out for a couple of hours for a drink with a girlfriend if he's going to be really late, whether to order a pizza to be delivered in an hour's time. It drives you crazy.

So, you hear the click of his key in the lock. In he comes.

Him: 'Sorry I'm late, darling.'

You: 'You're always bloody late.'

Him: 'Great. I get home after a really hard day, and all I get is grief.'

You: 'I'm surprised you bother to come home at all.'

There you are, off into a row.

The trouble is that you have made a very general (and aggressive) statement: 'You're always bloody late.' This could well be true, but he may see it as the nature of the job, and therefore something he can do nothing about. Indeed, he may feel his lateness is because he has to work so hard to make money for you both and (if you have them) the children.

It is far better to be specific in what you say. You need to put what's really concerning you in a clear form which can be tackled and negotiated. The conversation could have run this way:

Him: 'Hi, darling, I'm home. Sorry I'm a bit late.'

You: 'Hi, darling. Let's sit down and have a drink.'

When you're both comfortable (and any children are happily occupied and not screaming), you say: 'I want to talk to you about something that's upsetting me. It's that I never know when you're coming home.'

You then explain all about how you feel (never knowing when to cook, if to cook, whether to go out yourself, etc.).

Then suggest a practical solution.

Suggesting practical solutions

You can say you appreciate his work situation is complicated, but there must be ways to deal with it. Then you can put forward ideas. You might, for example, ask him to ring you every day in the late afternoon or very early evening (at home or at your work, as appropriate) to give you a rough estimate. Or, if he can't do that, ask him to ring as he's about to leave wherever he is so that you know he'll be home in half an hour. And you can say that if he's not rung at all by (say) 7.30, you'll regard yourself as free for the evening (to go out, invite friends over, eat, whatever you want to do and – if you have children – is practical).

The benefits for you of reaching such an arrangement are obvious; and there will be clear benefits for him too, which will encourage him in this new pattern of behaviour. Instead of coming home after a hard day to what he regards as an unjust earful, he will come home to a big hug – or an empty house followed a couple of hours later by a big hug.

It may be that this sort of practical solution will solve the problem; the only thing cheesing you off was the fact that his homecoming time was so erratic and unheralded. It was the lack of consideration which was getting to you. But if he's brought to see how you genuinely feel about it all and why, and acts to change matters, that might end the issue.

But maybe it isn't just the homecoming time that is the problem. Maybe you were complaining about that as a code for 'I'm miserable because your work seems to be more important to you than I am [and the kids]'.

This brings me to another major communication problem.

Subtexts

What people seem to be talking about isn't always *really* what they want to say. There's an unspoken subtext (or several), and that's the real issue.

We've all done it or been on the receiving end of it.

You: 'If your mother puts on her white gloves and runs a finger over our mantelpiece one more time I'll scream.'

Subtexts: well, she doesn't actually do that. But she does look round in a rather eagle-eyed fashion, and is of the generation which believes that dusters will shrivel her boy's manhood. You feel several things.

1 The truth is that you wish your partner would be a bit more assertive with her in terms of telling her the house is in fine nick, you organize things as you both want, and you do a red-hot job publishing books/raising children/being a steeplejack or whatever it is that you do. So he'd like a bit less of the unspoken criticism, and her offers to give you ironing lessons are quite unnecessary since he irons his own shirts, thanks.
2 His mother comes to lunch every Sunday. Given that you and your partner have little enough time together, this is a major slice out of that little time. He does it out of guilt and love, which of course you understand. But you don't want it to happen quite so often. An alternative might be that she comes every other Sunday, and on the

weeks she doesn't come he goes round on Tuesdays to her place for a coffee on his way home. He can tell her that he truly loves her but that for the sake of your marriage you need to spend more time together: but this is still a way he can see her once a week. This way he should satisfy his guilt and love, and your needs, and phrase it in such a way that his mother will not be hurt.

Both of these subtexts are serious and important issues, and both entirely obscured by the code about the mantelpiece. All that remark will have done is to annoy him for being unfair to and critical of his mother. Here's another example:

You: 'Your friend Steve is a drunken lout.'

Your partner is immediately on the defensive, as by insulting his friends you insult him too.

Subtext: he's not that bad, actually. What's really the matter is that your man is spending four evenings a week drinking with Steve and his cronies. You might be perfectly happy if he did it once or twice a week – but not *four* times, for goodness sake. You both will have things you want to do without the other, of course. It's just that for the sake of your relationship, if they're going to take a lot of time, it might be wiser to discuss it.

What your partner needs to know is how his being out so much makes you feel. He may genuinely not realize. He may just think you're being horrid about his friends. He may believe that spending a lot of time with mates is just something that men do, and shouldn't be a problem. You simply cannot assume that he fully understands your feelings and is therefore doing it in order to distress you.

You need to know why he does it, since that will be important in working out a solution which will satisfy you both. Is it a legacy from his pre-relationship-with-you days? Is he not keen to get home because he thinks you're going to get at him for something? (Which you will, because you're angry that he's been out with the lads *again*, which will make him even less keen to come home, so he stays out with the lads, and so on, round and round. . . .)

Coming clean over just one thing that upsets or angers you might also start a pattern of coming clean about other things too. The more you do it, the easier it will become.

Be very clear in expressing your emotions

To emphasize the fact that you must be very explicit about your emotions as well as your thoughts, let's look at an experiment which illustrates how subtle misunderstandings can be. Two German psychologists, Gisela Trommsdorff and Helga John, recruited thirty couples who had been living together for at least a year; the participants were aged between twenty and sixty-eight. One couple at a time discussed for fifteen minutes a topic of middling importance to them about which they disagreed. Typical conflicts were over 'visiting relatives; buying a piece of furniture; doing housework' (well, there's a shock). From a videotape of their discussion, each person picked out the 'most important statement' made by their partner.

Next, each statement was rated by the speaker in terms of their emotions when they made it and how they reckoned the listener reacted; and by the listener in terms of what they *thought* the speaker was feeling at the time and what the listener *actually* felt on hearing what was said. The ratings were of eighteen different emotions, ranging from anger, disappointment, sorrow and shame to affection, trust, interest and gladness.

From these measures the researchers were able to work out how correct each person was at interpreting the partner's emotions when he or she was speaking *and* listening.

The results showed clearly that women were more accurate than men. Being specifically instructed to focus on the other's feelings rather than on one's own during the discussion did increase accuracy for both sexes, but women were still better at decoding the other's emotions.

Women more than men have been brought up to be concerned with relationships, and this seems to have endless knock-on effects. There is, however, an alternative explanation to women's superiority in this department. The researchers speculate: 'Women maybe more skilled in masking certain emotions; they may communicate more indirectly or subtly and thereby make it more difficult for men to decode accurately.'

Either way, grasping a partner's feelings correctly is an area where it may not pay to be over-confident. At the very least, women can't always be sure that they're understood nor men that they understand. So forget emotional subtexts. Come right out with it.

Encouraging him to listen

But, of course, it's absolutely no use your coming clean if he doesn't listen. If you want someone to listen properly to what you're saying, you want to make sure of two things.

Make sure he's calm

First ensure he is sitting down somewhere comfortably and is calm. You don't want to broach something delicate when he's distracted and in a hurry, exhausted and tetchy, or stirred up about something that's happened in the day. If *you're* angry, try to wait until it's dissipated before you begin a sorting-out talk. Then you can tell him *calmly* that you're angry.

Preserve his self-esteem

Phrase what you want to say in terms of *your* thoughts and feelings about something specific which he has done. 'I feel X . . . (upset, rattled, insecure, angry, etc.) about Y (a specific action or statement by your partner)' is infinitely better than 'You are Z . . . (a bastard, mean, selfish, inconsiderate, etc.)' You'll get several quantum leaps further in terms of getting what you want.

Criticism and blame are not well received by most people. We don't, after all, enjoy having our self-esteem dented. So it's best to avoid criticism of the other *as a person*. This way, you preserve his self-esteem. It's more effective to say what you feel about a specific piece of behaviour; this is much less threatening than saying how *awful* he is as a person for having done it. Otherwise, if you put someone badly on the defensive, their most likely reaction is immediately to stop listening to you, to deny your accusations and to start attacking back. Or they may simply be very upset and hurt and walk off.

It is also wise to reserve your (carefully phrased) criticism for things which matter. Don't keep complaining about his preference for ancient Y-fronts rather than sassy silk boxers. Save it for his preference for spending all of every weekend lovingly polishing his motorbike. After all, no one is perfect, and your partner does not want to be made to feel a huge mass of wretched and irritating faults.

The five steps

So the message so far is:

1 make sure he's calm when you broach the subject
2 be specific, not general
3 suggest specific, practical solutions where possible
4 don't talk in code; reveal the true subtext
5 talk about 'I feel', not 'You are'

These techniques apply to positive things as well as negative ones, of course. Maybe it's not a problem like lateness which you want to broach. Perhaps it's that you want to go out and have fun more often – just the two of you.

You could:

get increasingly sulky and silent because you've been waiting for him to suggest taking you out for dinner for weeks, and you're wondering how long it's going to take him to think of it, the miserable sod. Or start saying things like: 'I think I'll give my only decent jacket to Oxfam'; or, 'Everything on the telly's rubbish these days.'

He might actually not have twigged at all what's wrong. He may be tired when he gets home and without thinking has settled into a routine. Couch potatoes could take his correspondence course, and his contribution to the feast of reason and the flow of soul is to grunt with the effort of pressing the buttons on the remote control. Hints may not be sufficient to transmit the true message.

You should:

follow steps 1–5 above, and *tell him.*

GETTING HIM TO COMMUNICATE

It's not good, however, your getting into the habit of coming clean if he refuses to play ball. He needs to be encouraged to reveal his thoughts and feelings to you.

For many people – men on average more than women – revealing their inner thoughts and feelings can sometimes be difficult. This may be especially true where what needs to be said is potentially threatening to the relationship or felt to be very embarrassing (sexual matters are often seriously blushmaking). Revealing vulnerability can be tricky, too. Men report being less likely to reveal certain negative emotions – depression, anxiety, anger and fear – to their partner than women do.

Yet you want him to talk. If there is something in the relationship, or about your behaviour, that is troubling him, *you need to know.* You also want him to talk about things that are troubling him which are nothing to do with the relationship. One of the strongest binding elements between two people is their ability to reveal things to each other. According to one study, the total amount of self-disclosure both given and received predicted very well which couples remained together over a four-year period. Other work, too, shows that increased self-disclosure is linked to higher satisfaction with the relationship. This assumes, of course, that what is revealed is either positive (about the partner and the relationship, anyway) or, if negative, is properly dealt with. Obviously, lots of self-disclosure about how your partner is simply a pain in the neck isn't going to help matters. But if your partner is currently feeling that you *are* being a pain in the neck, you do need to know exactly what's wrong so that it *can* be dealt with properly.

Whichever way you look at it, he's got to talk. So what can you do?

Encourage by example

By consistently following the five steps listed above, another advantage should be that you set an example for *him* to follow. Revealing your own feelings may act as a 'model' that your partner might start to imitate.

You can help him overtly, too. You can tell him what you're doing, and suggest he tries it next time he's got something bugging him, or that he wants.

Reward

When he does reveal a difficult thought or feeling, reward him for it.

Him: 'I do wish we didn't have to have your friend Sally round. She can't stop talking about her ghastly relationships and her gynaecological problems and she drives me crazy.'

You: 'I'm really glad you told me. I know she does that, and I don't mind so much because we've known each other so long. We used to get the school bus together and pinch the boys' caps. I'll make sure in future that I see her on my own or in a large group so you don't have to talk to her.'

This is a far better response than: 'How *dare* you be rude about my friend. What about your friend John? The one who keeps dropping cigarette ash all over the carpet? Have I ever said a single word about him?' (If you hadn't, by the way, and it upset you that much, you should have done! Calmly. . . .)

Probe

When you think he's talking in generalities, or in code, you can encourage him to reveal all by gentle questioning. If what he says seems very general, ask for specifics. If you suspect that the fact he's started criticizing your clothes is code for something else, then gently probe as to what it might be.

When he hints at subterranean dark thoughts, don't let it go by because you're terrified of what they are. Ferret about a bit.

Him: 'Oh, you're working late at the mag *again*? I'm a magazine widower!' (laughs)

You: 'Darling, is this getting to you? Let's talk. Tell me.'

Actively listen

If he has started to tell you what's on his mind, it's absolutely crucial to *listen* to what he's saying. The truth is that we often don't listen properly. We're too busy planning what *we're* going to say. Sometimes, too, we can be so whipped up in a maelstrom of our own emotions that we don't take it in.

The secret here is to try to concentrate on your partner's feelings rather than your own, and to engage yourself fully in what the other person is saying by 'active listening':

1 Ask questions.
2 A *very* important technique if the issue is complex or difficult or ambiguous in any way: state back to him, in your own

words, what you think he's said. 'So, you feel I'm seeing too much of my friends and not enough of you / being deliberately obstructive by not hand-darning your socks / being irritating by ringing the office to remind you to pick up a bag of cat litter on your way home?' This has several advantages:

a It enables you to check out that you *have* actually understood what he's saying. Because we don't always. How often have we heard the cry, 'Oh no, I didn't mean *that!*'

b It enables the other person to hear what the words they're saying sound like. Sometimes, when you hear what you're saying repeated back to you, you realize that actually it *is* a bit unfair, not strictly true or not quite what you meant to say.

c It will make the other person feel that you really are listening to him, and you definitely are trying to understand. Indeed, once you've got what he said right he'll be reassured that you *do* understand. This does not mean that you will in the end agree with him, but it is very important that he should feel he has the right to express his views. You might even sometimes want to say things like 'I can see why you think that, but actually I. . . .' Obviously such phrases should not be over-used, however, or they will sound insincere.

The point is that we all want to feel we have the right to express how we feel and not be automatically squashed for it. It's OK for someone to counter-argue, but not to imply that our opinion is of no worth or interest – or, indeed, that we are stupid even to think such a thing.

Communicating well is something that couples really need to do in order to keep going happily. Your man in particular may need some encouragement in this department; a survey of four hundred therapists revealed that the largest single reason they thought marriages failed was the husband's inability to communicate his feelings.

The ability to communicate becomes of absolutely critical importance when a couple is in conflict.

DEALING WITH CONFLICT

This is an extraordinarily tricky business, yet it is an essential skill. Failing to deal with it satisfactorily is very likely, over time, to eat away at the fabric of your relationship like dry rot.

Good and bad techniques

There are several main ways in which you and your partner might choose to deal with conflict when it rears its ugly head. Dutch psychologist Bram Buunk and his colleagues, for instance, have analysed five:

Aggression
Verbal attack.

Avoidance
Either leaving the room, or avoiding discussing it.

Soothing
'There, there, dear.' Trying to smooth matters over without actually talking about the problem.

Compromise
Trying to find what sounds like a fair solution – but without fully discussing the underlying issues.

Problem solving
Discussing feelings directly and openly; exploring the causes of the conflict; and searching for a mutually satisfactory solution.

Let's see how these might work.

He says: 'I don't want your idle, layabout brother to come and live with us while he "looks for work". His idea of looking for work is to lie in bed until five o'clock and then say, "Oh dear, I suppose the Jobcentre'll be shut by now."'

You say:

1 'Don't you say that about my brother! He's family, and he's damn well coming whether you want him or not. And what about your bloody mother – ringing you all hours of the day and night because her over-fed moggie keeps getting stuck halfway through the catflap?'
2 Nothing, you're too busy slamming the door on your way out.
3 'Sweetheart, don't get upset. It's nothing worth getting upset over. I'm terribly sorry – he won't stay long I'm sure.'
4 'What about him staying six months, and if he hasn't found a job by then he'll have to go?'
5 'Tell me what it is that most upsets you. Is it that you don't like him at all? Do you *truly* think he's just sponging on us and won't make any effort to find a job? Is it that you think he'll just try to stay forever?' You go on to tell him how you feel about your brother, and by talking it all through you reach a solution that is satisfactory to you both. Perhaps you agree on what your brother must do each day to find work, and agree to review the situation every week with an outside time limit.

Well, put like this, anyone with a brain larger than a peanut would see that approach 5 – problem solving – was the best method of dealing with conflict. And the psychological research evidence supports that conclusion.

But the fact remains that although, like many other aspects of relationships, it seems pretty obvious when you look at it, so many of us don't. Who among us could swear that we'd never dealt with conflict by using techniques 1–3? At least technique 4 isn't bad – it's just that 5 is better. It's also the case that sometimes we see that there is a conflict present – and yet neither of us mentions it at all. We hope, fearfully, that the problem will just Go Away. But it won't, and so it just festers.

Patterns in good and bad relationships

An extremely likely scenario when a couple are dealing badly with conflict is a pattern of attack and immediate retaliation, setting up extremely negative (and sometimes repetitive) cycles. But angry rows and yelling make people feel worse, not better because they've 'let it out'. Downward spirals of attack and counter-attack are a distinguishing feature of unhappy marriages.

According to the evidence, there are two quite distinct patterns of communication and conflict management in happy and distressed partnerships. In happy marriages, compared to unhappy ones, there tends to be:

- more talk
- more self-disclosure (in both depth and breadth)
- clear, direct messages without hidden meanings
- active listening skills
- more agreement
- more expressions of love, approval, affection, encouragement, respect and esteem
- more emotional support
- more positive statements and fewer negative ones (including criticism)
- a greater likelihood of interpreting the partner's behaviour as positive
- greater ability to express feelings about a marital problem in a neutral manner
- more sensitivity to each other's feelings
- more use of idiosyncratic codes (e.g. private jokey phrases for sex – 'let's go swing on a chandelier' type of thing. . . .)

- more laughter
- more positive 'non-verbal communication' (warm tone of voice, touches, etc.)

Also:

- most matters, including intimate ones, are discussed
- happy couples convey to each other the feeling that each understands what the other says to them

In unhappy marriages, in comparison, there is:

- more negative behaviour, both verbal (such as criticism) and non-verbal (such as lack of touching)
- fewer positive actions, such as being affectionate and supportive
- fewer attempts to solve problems and exchange information
- a greater likelihood that negative behaviour on the part of one partner will be reciprocated by the other
- a lower ratio of agreements to disagreements
- more conflict and longer-lasting 'scenes'
- more coercion

What's more:

- one spouse is often significantly more dominant than the other in conversation
- statements by the spouse are interpreted as being more negative than the speaker intended
- discussions are more likely to start out with complaints which then trigger an escalating cycle of negative exchanges – 'You're a sod', 'You're a nag' – with each partner repeating their position again and again.

Emergency action

If you feel you are at risk of descending into the downward spirals which seem to be a hallmark of unhappy relationships, there is something you can do *immediately*, before you start practising the communication and conflict skills described earlier. Just stop automatically lashing back when he says something you don't like.

Evidence is growing that a crucial element in successful relationships is the way you react when your partner does or says something potentially destructive. For example, he is irritable or unkind, or behaves inconsiderately. 'Well, I don't see why I can't put my coffee mug down on this month's *Vogue*.'

Research by American psychologists Nancy Yovetich and Caryl Rusbult has found that, when women and men are asked to say what they'd do if a partner behaved badly, they're more likely to respond destructively if asked to re-spond fast. But a pause of as little as six seconds was enough to make people react more constructively. It's not just a matter of 'calming down'; it's that those vital few seconds are enough to enable you to *weigh up the possible consequences* of following your inclination to fight fire with fire.

People's automatic impulse is often to lash back, even to a loved partner. This is probably, the researchers point out, because being nice at this point might seem humiliating. As we've seen, one of the signs of a disintegrating relationship is that the couple in question get into cycles of say-some-thing-negative/say-something-negative-right-back. In happy relationships, people seem more likely to inhibit the impulse to retaliate. This gives them a better chance of sorting things out and/or not making mountains out of molehills. In fact, responding in a calm, caring and constructive manner is a sign of strength, not weakness.

So next time your partner says something that could trigger a quarrel, take a few seconds before replying. If necessary, say something like, 'I'll put the kettle on, then we can talk about this' or nip to the loo. You won't need long to decide what to do – to tackle what lies behind it, or perhaps to conclude that the outburst was rare enough to be put down to exhaustion after a bad day. (After all, if that's all it is, the poor man doesn't want to be made even more exhausted by a totally unnecessary 'What's *really* wrong?' session!)

Male avoidance of conflict

Another common pattern in relationships which are in difficulty is that the woman is aggressively conflict-engaging, while the man withdraws and avoids confrontation. Presumably his refusal to talk about it is driving her into a fury of frustration.

A number of studies have found that men avoid confronting marital conflict more than women do. This seems strange, given that men are stereotypically the aggressive and dominant ones. So why does it happen?

Male avoidance could be partly because confronting problems in relationships involves talking about negative feelings, which they often find less easy than women do. But we also now have another clue.

American psychologists Robert Levenson, Laura Carstensen and John Gottman asked two groups of couples, who had been married either for at least fifteen, or at least thirty-five years, to try to resolve a conflict in their relationship. Discussing problems can make people feel angry, sad or fearful, and this raises their levels of physiological arousal. So while the couples talked, the researchers carefully monitored their bodily signals such as heart rate.

They found that in both groups, the men reported feeling more negative the more aroused they were. For the women, there was no connection between the emotions they recorded and their arousal levels.

There is some general evidence that men are more attuned to changes in their bodily states than women are. It may be, the researchers suggest, that men try to avoid conflict – or end it quickly – because they find high arousal levels very unpleasant. Women may not be so conscious of how aroused they are, or not feel badly when they are aroused, or both. So they're more likely to keep pushing for a resolution.

If this explanation is right, it adds an extra dimension of importance to the 'keep him calm' element of the communication skills I've been discussing. If you want to talk over a problem with your partner, it's important to try to wait until he's feeling relaxed, and then keep him that way as far as possible. So don't start to discuss it if he's already in a stew about something else, don't rip his newspaper out of his hands and yell 'Listen to me, blast you!', and don't churn him into a lather by attacking his character. You don't want him dashing to the door or raising the newspaper barrier so that he can bring down his arousal levels.

The 5:1 ratio

Psychologist John Gottman has done a great deal of research on marriages, and has found something very important: that in stable marriages, 'positivity' outweighed 'negativity' in the ratio of about 5:1. In unstable marriages, it was less than 1:1. The point is clear. You're going to get some disagreements, arguments, criticism and the like in a relationship; but what's important is that this is heavily outweighed by positive interactions (agreement, complimenting, hugging, humour, etc.). So if you *do* have the odd unpleasant interchange, check that you're getting the overall *balance* right.

Is poor communication down to dissatisfaction?

You might think that the reason for unhappy couples' communication being so bad is that they got fed up with each other, and were communicating fine beforehand. However, while it's true that feeling fed up will make communication and problem solving harder, the evidence is that poor communication and conflict management can also affect how happy you are in the relationship.

It would be wrong to suggest that improving communication will guarantee a happy partnership. It may just point up the fact that there are vast and irreconcilable differences between you. But if this is so, it is probably better to know than to spend decades in sniping misery. In any case, researchers think it is more likely that good communication will serve to bind you together, increasing intimacy and reducing misunderstandings and conflicts. It is certainly, as we have seen, a hallmark of happy marriages.

VIOLENCE

So far, I have been using the word 'attack' in a verbal sense. But in some relationships, the attack is physical. Sometimes both men and women push and shove each other in anger and frustration – it hardly needs me to point out that this is *not* the way to solve problems. If that is happening in your relationship, you need to start practising some verbal techniques fast; and leave the room to calm yourself down if necessary, and to allow him to calm down, before talking about it.

Most serious of all is the case where a partner hits and hurts the other. It is far more often the man who beats up his partner than the woman who beats up the man, although the latter does sometimes occur. If you are being physically abused, this I regard as an exception to what I have been saying about the vital importance of talking things through. In this instance, only drastic action will serve. Because of the sex difference in the frequency of spouse-beating, and because most research has been done on 'wife batterers', in the advice that follows I shall assume that the man is the attacker.

If your man hits you, is he full of remorse afterwards? Does he say he'll never do it again? Do you believe him each time?

If so, then your experience is typical. Wife-beaters are often extremely manipulative. What is so insidious about this situation is that, during his remorseful and loving patches, you think you're getting a glimpse of the 'real man'.

You then think that if only certain aspects of your lives changed, he'd be like that all the time. You think, perhaps, that if *you* were different, he wouldn't hit you. Or if the children were quieter he wouldn't hit you. Or if he had a job he wouldn't hit you. Or – a common thought, this – if he drank less he wouldn't hit you.

You might believe that alcohol is the cause of the problem, by breaking down his inhibitions and leading to 'out-of-character' behaviour. But in fact, it's now thought that wife-beaters often drink to *provide an excuse* for becoming violent. They know that, when drunk, people are supposed to be 'not responsible' for what they do. So when they want to get violent, they get drunk first. This accounts for the fact that they are also perfectly capable of hitting their partners when sober.

Essentially, all these 'if X changed all would be well' thoughts are delusions. What can be terribly hard to accept is that what he's like when he's violent *is the 'real man' too*. The causes of his behaviour are deep-rooted.

A partner who beats you is trying to exert control over you. He thinks that's what being a man is about. He probably has low self-esteem, and being abusive is the only way he feels able to 'keep you in line'. He has very probably come from an abusive background himself. Either he saw his father hitting his mother, and/or he was physically abused as a child himself. So he has come to believe that violence is the way for a man to control members of his family. Because he is so insecure himself – and probably regards you as his possession – he may be appallingly jealous.

Don't fall into the trap of the 'rescue fantasy', either. What I mean by this is the dangerous romantic myth that you can redeem him by your love.

There are only two things that will alter matters:

1 He accepts full responsibility for his own behaviour, and recognizes that he has a problem.
2 He seeks some professional therapeutic help based on a true desire for change.

If he will not do these things, for your own sake you need to get out of the relationship. If you have children, you need to get out for their sake too. Men who abuse their wives often do the same to their offspring.

To end the relationship, of course, is usually not an easy matter. Being physically abused by a partner can do dreadful things to a woman's self-esteem (which in some cases may not have been very high in the first place). He may also have subjected you to emotional abuse – such as verbally humiliating you in public – which will have compounded the problem. So you may fear that you can't manage on your own, that no one will love you in the future, and all sorts of paralysing thoughts which are quite wrong. You may have been reduced to the state where you find it difficult to make decisions or long-term plans.

Women in such situations are often also at home with children, and feel economically dependent and trapped. To make matters worse, they very often have not told anyone, so they feel terribly isolated. Indeed, their partner may have tried deliberately to isolate them from their friends.

The first move is to start telling people and recruiting their support and practical help: family, any friends still left to you, and relevant professional agencies (see Further Reading for a helpful book). You loved someone who turned out to have a severe problem. *You* were not the cause of his problem. The change will be difficult, but what price spending the rest of your life dreading the turning of the front door key in the lock?

You must take sensible steps to protect yourself in the long as well as the short term, which you will be able to do when you have social support and professional advice as to how to deal with the situation. You may also need professional advice on means of financial support, accommodation, whether you need retraining, finding work and so on.

Change is always hard. But to build a life free of fear and pain is worth it; as is the burgeoning of your self-esteem that will gradually, let us hope, follow.

Conflict is going to be unavoidable in any relationship. What matters is how both partners deal with it. In couples where no one's beating anyone else up, you *can* deal with it through talk.

4

Powering

The trouble with the great romantic myths of the binding power of love is that they don't address the nitty-gritty. Dante, for example, never exchanged more than courteous greetings with Beatrice. They never got to the stage of having to work out how to live together and to negotiate which way round to hang the medieval equivalent of a loo roll.

In every relationship, as it ticks on day-to-day, there will be rewards and costs. To power it along and keep you both happy, your rewards need to be higher than your costs; and so do his. You won't manage it every day, of course, nor should you be anxiously totting up the score every night! But on balance, over time, you both need to feel that the relationship is rewarding more than the reverse.

Of course, many people do stay in a relationship in which they're not happy. This can be for many reasons: the presence of children, feeling economically dependent, thinking you've invested so much already in the relationship over the years, fear that you'll never find an alternative partner.

However, my concern is that relationships between two people should be happy, not just long. Who wants to spend years gritting their teeth or sunk in a sea of emotional mediocrity?

It is also the case that, even though unhappy relationships can keep going for a long time for various reasons, the chances are that they'll crack apart in the end. Today, social pressures against divorce are minimal compared to those that acted on previous generations.

But what is rewarding and costly in a relationship?

REWARDS AND COSTS

For each of us, what we find rewarding in a relationship will be an idiosyncratic set of elements. The same is true of our partner. What is crucial is that we *know* what our partner finds rewarding; and that we transmit to him what we find rewarding.

What is astonishing is how often people don't tell you directly. They may drop hints, and will probably reply if asked directly, and one can deduce things by watching their behaviour. But a person's true feelings about the way they're living their lives are often not straightforwardly expressed.

How often, too, have you heard a friend, recently left by her partner, say, 'I never *realized* how he felt about the way we were living our lives until his speech telling me he was going. I suppose, looking back, there were clues, but I didn't pick up on them. . . .'

In an ideal world, of course, he would have told you in time to rectify the situation. But that doesn't always seem to happen.

So you need to discover what he finds rewarding.

His rewards

There are various methods of finding out what they are.

1 Ask him. Don't dismiss this as too pathetically obvious for words. If it's so obvious, why don't all couples do it as a matter of course and thus do their bit towards lowering the divorce rate?

- ask him what activities he enjoys doing – leisure and sexual
- ask him what he most likes to do in the first half-hour or an hour after work. (Maybe he wants half an hour to unwind before even talking or moving)
- ask him about his favourite food
- ask him which of your friends he likes best
- ask him which of your relatives he likes best
- ask him what he'd like you to do that you're not doing
- ask him what he'd like you to do more of
- ask him what's not happening in your lives together that he'd like to happen

Do you – with *absolute certainty* – know what your current partner would say? Or, if you're not with anyone at the moment, your last partner?

If you do, give yourself a gold star. The rest of us probably need to find out.

2 Watch out for clues.

> *Him*: 'Wasn't that fascinating, what Charles and Jane were telling us about tarpon fishing in the Gulf of Mexico? We never do *anything* like that.'
>
> *You* (*distracted*): 'Eerm, no. Blast – what's that burnt smell coming from the oven?'

3 Watch his behaviour. Well, what exactly is it that brings the biggest smile to his face? Being pounced on and dragged to bed? Being told you love him? A really relaxing, self-indulgent evening involving a delivered curry and an Arnold Schwarzenegger video? Or what?

His costs

You need to know about his 'costs' (the opposite of rewards) too.

1 Ask him what irritates him, angers him, depresses him. Does he feel dragged down by having so many rituals and

routines in your lives together? Upset that he's always the one who makes the sexual moves? Annoyed by the fact that, whenever you're invited to spend an evening with his friends, you always groan meaningfully?

2 Watch out for clues. Sometimes people do give us clues to what's troubling them, but we don't pick them up because we misattribute the motives behind what they're saying. If they burst out with, 'God, why do your friends ring up every five seconds?' you might put it down to irritation after a bad day. If they chortle and say, when you've had a really busy few weeks at work, 'Darling, is that you? I hardly recognized you!' you might assume it's just a joke.

You might be right on both counts. But you may not. The thing to watch out for is repetition. Repeated irritation, jokes and mild remarks are serious clues, and will need to be followed up by you. (Remember the issue of 'uneasy feelings'? It's very important not to ignore them.)

3 Watch his behaviour. What habitually brings a frown to his face? What triggers off unusually quiet periods? What sort of event does he frequently miss because he has to 'work late' or 'fix that leaking pipe' (going to musicals with your mother, accompanying you to dinner parties with your old school pals, that sort of thing . . .)?

I am not suggesting that you raise his reward level and lower his cost level with no regard to your own feelings. But very often, such raising/lowering can be done at no – or little – cost to yourself once you've twigged what he relishes/dislikes. Indeed, in the process you might get more rewards yourself. Maybe you shouldn't dismiss big-game fishing in such a cavalier fashion; and if he's going to be more cheerful, that'll be nice for you too.

Compromise can also be a good move; after all, perhaps you needn't drag him to those jolly dinners with your old school friends *quite* so frequently. And who knows, the new Ibsen production he's bursting to see might be hugely appreciated by your mother. It's just that everyone assumes that because she likes musicals she doesn't like anything else.

In my view, we often make too many assumptions in our dealings with each other.

Of course, it's not just his rewards and costs in the relationship that are important. What about yours?

Your rewards

1 Tell him what pleases you. Normally that's the sort of advice that's given in a purely sexual context – and of course it is vital to tell him what turns you on (more of this anon).

You also need to let him know when he *does* do something you like. On the too-rare occasions, say, when he remarks how gorgeous you look, you can say, 'Oh, *thank you* – I love it when you say things like that.' Or when he gives you jewellery instead of French iron casseroles for your birthday. Or tells you he loves you. Or takes you out to dinner as a surprise. Or suggests an outing that you would both enjoy. Or. . . .

Don't, of course, always use the same form of words to reward him – that would sound formulaic and insincere. It is also a fact that, if something is repeated often, we become accustomed to it and cease to notice it. Therefore repetitive phrases will lose their power to reward.

Just let him know, somehow, how happy these things make you. The truth is that, however crude it sounds, we are likely to do more of what we are rewarded for.

2 On the question of clues, these, as I've said, can often be missed or understood. The only clues I'd advocate for increasing your rewards would lie in your non-verbal behaviour. When he does something you like, you can reward him verbally – as in the 'love it when you say things like that' example above. But you can also do it non-verbally – by hugging, kissing, giving him huge, happy, rewarding grins and so on.

3 Ways of behaving. Sometimes you may have to 'model' the behaviour you want from him. Perhaps you'd love

him, just once, to take you out to dinner somewhere a bit more exciting than the Chinese down the road with the shares in monosodium glutamate. So *you* choose somewhere, book it as a surprise, and when he's thoroughly enjoying himself over the rare steak and pommes frites tell him it's his turn to do this next!

The essential point is to remember that, however much he loves you, he does not have telepathic access to the contents of your brain.

Your costs

1 Please, please tell him, for goodness' sake. In Chapter 3 I talked about ways in which you can say difficult things to him in the most effective way. Don't think that you won't mention what's upsetting you because you can't face it and would rather have an easy life. If something that he repeatedly does – or doesn't – do, and which isn't a trivial matter, is driving you demented/depressing or upsetting you, you must raise the issue. Even at the cost of A Difficult Talk, better that than continuing to feel as you do. Because it probably won't get better, it'll get worse – you'll build up a head of steam like a pressure cooker, and explode. So tell him how unhappy it makes you that he never tells you how he feels about you unless you say it first. That he always leaves the loo seat up. That he thinks washing up liquid will be unkind to his hands.

2 Clues – don't risk it. Chances are he won't pick them up.

3 Your behaviour. You could imitate what he does that irritates you. Leave the washing-up for forty-eight hours so he can see exactly what things would be like if you didn't always do it. Get home from work, pick up the newspaper, flop in front of the TV, say you're too tired to cook and when's dinner?

I wouldn't advocate over-use of this technique, however. Talking, I believe, is likely to bring the best outcome. But if you believe it necessary, a single behavioural demonstration of what you see the problem to be might at least focus his mind, and make it clear how strongly you feel. *Then* you can talk about it.

FAIRNESS

The rewards you give your partner are part of your 'input' into the relationship. Your input consists of *everything* you put into the relationship from, say, financial contributions and practical efforts on the domestic front to your time, love and loyalty. Some of these things may not even be seen as rewarding to the other person – he may simply take them for granted. Nevertheless, they are all contributions which you are making to the relationship.

You also receive certain outcomes from the relationship yourself. These are not only things which seem obviously rewarding, but also the more subtle rewards of, for instance, a deep-rooted feeling of security and the knowledge that you're not going to be the one who has to get the spider out of the bath.

Your partner, too, has input into and outcomes from the relationship.

So let's look at something which, if not tackled early on, can lead to a slow build-up of anger and resentment.

People are more likely to be satisfied if their relationship is *fair and equitable* in terms of inputs and outcomes. Dutch psychologists Nico Van Yperen and Bram Buunk have asked members of couples who were married or cohabiting: 'Considering what you put into your relationship compared to what you get out of it, and what your partner puts in compared to what (s)he gets out of it, how does your relationship "stack up"?' Their answers could range from 'I am getting a much better deal than my partner' through to 'My partner is getting a much better deal than I am.'

Obviously there can be lots of 'exchange elements' in a relationship: being nice to be with, sexual needs, domestic chores and so on. But this study found three to be particularly important for both sexes when they're working out how equitable their relationship is:

- commitment to the relationship
- being sociable and pleasant to be with
- being attentive and thoughtful

Feelings of inequity can affect satisfaction with the relationship (being under-benefited is, of course, a more serious problem than the inequity of feeling very over-benefited and consequently guilty).

Most likely, these researchers believe, people would prefer their relationship to be equitable because each partner's inputs and outputs are roughly equal. This sounds more desirable than a situation where the relationship is equitable in the sense of the *ratios* of inputs and outcomes being equal, but where this is achieved by one partner putting in a lot and getting a lot out, whereas the other puts in little and gets little.

If you *are* conscious of a sense of unfairness, as with rewards and costs, this issue too may have to be discussed openly. In this study, in 40 per cent of the couples one or both of the partners did not agree on who was deprived, over-benefited or equitably treated. They hadn't twigged how the partner felt.

Van Yperen and Buunk point out that equity seems to be more important to some than to others. Perhaps, for some people, it's outweighed by other things. There's evidence that the absolute level of rewards you're receiving in the relationship affects satisfaction more than equity does. So perhaps if you feel amply rewarded, you don't start looking at the relationship in terms of each person's relative inputs and outcomes.

COMMON REWARDS

Those three elements that people seem to take particularly into account when they judge if the relationship is equitable or not (commitment, sociability and pleasantness, attentiveness and thoughtfulness) look to me like very important rewards. While the precise set of an individual's rewards and costs will be idiosyncratic, it is also true that many of us would agree that certain things are definitely rewarding (or, indeed, that their absence is costly).

These particular three factors can manifest themselves in a relationship in many different ways. A person's commitment to you might appear in expressions of love; sociability and pleasantness in making an effort to enjoy leisure and conversation; attentiveness and thoughtfulness in trying hard to put themselves in your shoes and acting accordingly. If you've just come in after a stressful meeting, they bring you a cup of coffee and wait half an hour before telling you that your favourite hamster has gone to the great cage in the sky.

There was also a fourth element highlighted in the 'equity' study. One of the additional areas mentioned by women (but not men) who felt deprived was: 'spending more time accomplishing housekeeping tasks'. Well, I bet you're amazed about that! In fact, 25 per cent of the women in this study felt they were being short-changed overall, whereas only 13 per cent of the men did.

So let's now look more closely at a selection of elements in a relationship which are widely regarded as rewarding (and, in varying degrees, likely to feed into many people's 'equity' calculations): expressions of love; satisfaction with leisure, conversation and other lifestyle factors; having a partner who takes your perspective; a fair division of domestic chores.

Expressions of love

In a relationship that's been going on for some time, there is a great danger that expressions of love to your partner will go into a decline. After all, you've committed yourself, haven't you – what else do you need to do, for heaven's sake?

One study illustrates the point in a rather alarming manner. Looking at changes in the frequency of affectionate behaviour in the first year of 'wedded bliss', it transpired that saying 'I love you' dropped by 44 per cent, approval and compliments by 30 per cent, doing something nice for the partner by 28 per cent, and sharing physical affection (other than intercourse) by 39 per cent. All these activities are ways of expressing love and affection.

The trouble is that, as Robert Sternberg has pointed out, if love is not expressed, it can become weaker. If you express your love, you remind yourself that you feel it and you give it a boost. Our actions do affect our feelings. What's more, if you don't express your love in actions, there is a risk that your partner will become distressed. That, in turn, will feed back and potentially damage your relationship.

So there is a danger that one or both of you will slow down drastically in the 'expressions of love' department (if it drops that much in the first year of marriage, after five years it might be through the floor). And if one of you rarely expresses your love for the other, the other is hardly going to feel encouraged to keep on expressing their feelings solo. So you might get into a feedback cycle in which you might mention that you love each other at Christmas and on birthdays.

A complicating factor is that people can express their love in different ways. For one person, polishing your shoes might be an expression of love; for another, 'I'll love you passionately, darling, until the seas run dry' might be the only acceptable demonstration.

The risk here is obvious. The partner of the shoe-polisher might have no idea that this is the s-p's way of telling you how he feels. The partner of the 'I love you so . . .' declaimer might think, 'Well, yeah, words are easy. But when was the last time she left work before eight o'clock so she could be with me?'

Love can be expressed in many ways. Just look at the list of actions that drop in the first year of marriage.

- saying it in words
- saying things that are loving, such as 'How handsome/ gorgeous you look, sweetheart' in a warm and intimate tone of voice
- *doing* things that are loving. Polishing your shoes, buying the latest book by your favourite cartoonist as a non-Christmas present, arranging a surprise party for your birthday. Most importantly, clearly making the relationship a priority and making time to be together
- non-verbal loving; hugging and kissing without it always being a prelude to sex

If individuals differ in the way they express love, their partner might not twig; and the individuals might start to feel unloved themselves. One tiny study – of only seven couples – is worth mentioning here. In social scientific terms, findings from such a small sample shouldn't have too much weight placed upon them; but it does illustrate this point about individual differences perfectly. It also raises the possibility that men and women may often differ in their expressions of love.

In this study, the women wanted their husbands to express their love and affection verbally. Their husbands, in contrast, liked their wives to do something positive in the 'instrumental' department (for example, to cook a good meal). They seemed to see instrumental actions as expressions of love and affection. Indeed, when the researchers told one man to be more affectionate, he decided to wash his wife's car. Unfortunately, however, neither the researchers nor, crucially, his wife, saw this as an affectionate act.

This sex difference does seem very plausible. In another study, researchers asked partners in both dating and newly married couples about what they wanted to happen in a sexual relationship. In both types of couples, the thing that women wanted more than men was for their partners to *talk lovingly* more often than they did. (The men more than the women wanted more arousing sex.) The men in these samples would like more loving talk too, but not as much as the women.

Just looking around and listening to people, it also seems to me that men are more likely than women to say, 'Well, I'm here, aren't I?' Or, 'Well, I phoned, didn't I?' Or, 'I work hard to support my family. Would I be doing that if I didn't love them?' But to a partner, these sorts of actions might not be interpreted as love.

So, given the potential risks and misunderstandings, it might be worth asking yourself several rather hard questions.

- What do I say to express my love to my partner?
- What do I *do* to express that love?
- How does he interpret my words? Does he place weight on what I say?
- How does he interpret my actions? Does he see that I'm doing these things out of love, or might he be placing some other interpretation on them? For instance, if I've arranged a surprise party for him, does he realize I've done it out of love, or might he just think that I've done it because I personally enjoy giving parties?

The same questions can be asked the other way round.

- What does he say to me about his feelings?
- What does he do that could possibly be expressions of love?
- How do I interpret his words?
- How do I interpret his actions?

If you think about it carefully, you may see that there's a discrepancy between how you want him to take your words and actions and how he does take them; and between what he may be intending to convey to you and how *you're* taking it.

After all, if he thinks repairing a tap that irritates you is an expression of love and you don't, there is a danger of a misunderstanding developing of major proportions. As you storm out of the door with your suitcase he could be crying, 'But of *course* I love you, I thought you knew that. . . .'

So it's very important that (using the communicating and getting-him-to-talk skills I described earlier):

1 You ask him to put himself in your shoes, and to say what in his behaviour you should interpret as indicating love. (His presence, his financial contribution, cooking, feeding the budgie whose hungry squawking he knows you hate, or what?)
2 You convey to him what you need/would like in the way of loving words and actions.
3 You tell him that when you say you love him you mean it; and when you have to stay late for an urgent meeting it doesn't mean you don't love him and you really do try to keep that to a minimum; and when you hand him a glass of wine and don't speak for fifteen minutes when he gets in late and exhausted you're doing it out of love.
4 You ask him what he needs or would like in order to make him feel loved.

Because you don't want *him* storming out with a suitcase saying 'I know you kept telling me you loved me, but you were never *there* for me.'

Adored vs. understood

One word of warning. Once you're in a committed relationship, expressions of love in which you constantly tell him that he's utterly perfect may not – surprising as this seems – always be what he wants to hear.

An American study by psychologist William Swann and his colleagues has compared dating and married couples. Members of the dating couples clearly did want lots of 'stroking'. The more highly their partner thought of them (on aspects such as their intellect, attractiveness and social skills), the more intimate and satisfactory the relationship.

And this held true whatever their personal opinion of themselves.

But after marriage, there seems to be a shift. Married people felt most intimate when their spouse *saw them as they saw themselves*. If the partner *over*-rated them (or under-rated them, of course!) they felt less comfortable with the relationship. This happened even if they thought pretty well of themselves in the first place.

Dating, the researchers say, is a time when we want the other person to think we're great. But once you each feel you've 'passed the test' and the relationship has become long-term, it becomes more important to feel understood than to be uncritically adored. A partner who recognizes both your strengths and your weaknesses is in a better position to help you develop your unique potential and reach your goals in life.

There's one snag for the married men and women who thought badly of themselves. They felt more intimate with a spouse who thought rather badly of them too. In this case, unfortunately, their partner's behaviour might just serve to keep their self-esteem squashed.

So what should you do? If your partner has a fairly solid sense of self-worth, it's fine to praise him as long as you don't keep overdoing it in an unbelievable way. But if he has a poor self-image, it probably won't help to tell him he's absolutely wrong about his cooking abilities, shyness and clumsiness. It might be better to admit that, yes, he *is* a bit lethal in the kitchen, quiet at parties and worrying near china, but he has other hot assets and you love him anyway.

Lifestyle

I believe that lifestyle factors – how organized into set routines your life is; whether or not you have fun in your leisure time; whether or not you enjoy doing similar things and each other's company – can be of crucial importance in determining how well your relationship is going to go.

Boredom and routine

So, how is your life? Are Monday, Tuesday and Wednesday couch potato nights? Is it the weekly big shop at the supermarket on Thursday evenings? An Indian take-away on Fridays? Sex on Saturdays? Lunch with the in-laws on Sundays? Don't underestimate the dulling, undermining effects of routine, predictability and boredom. Psychologists believe that it can lead to 'emotional deadening'.

In the early stages of relationships, there's lots of uncertainty and unpredictability. Your emotions are kept on their toes and whirled about. But as the relationship continues, both partners commit themselves and life settles down into a predictable pattern, your emotions quieten down too. They can be aroused by novel events – for example, finding out your spouse is having an affair would wake them up a bit – but clearly such events don't always do your relationship a power of good.

But while you might not want your emotions to lie down in a stupor, you probably don't want to live through the years of your relationship with never a dull moment either. What relationships probably need, according to American psychologist Charles Berger, is both predictability and uncertainty. You need predictability in the central elements of the relationship to keep it stable. That is, you need to feel that he loves you, will stay with you, will care for you when you're ill, won't run off with his secretary. But you both need some novelty and excitement in the more peripheral areas of life.

So, to prevent the corrosion of routine and boredom, you can tackle it in two ways.

1 Examine the routine nature of your life as it is now.

It may be that the routine isn't strictly necessary. Sainsbury's on Thursdays might be a good move because it's late night shopping and you can get it out of the way for the week. But perhaps, instead of going home, putting away the shopping and slaving over a hot stove and collapsing, you could plan post-shopping treats. Whatever you fancy: sex, videos, take-away pasta. And maybe you could occasionally junk the shopping in favour of a riotous night out.

If you always have sex on the same day, don't. Live dangerously and try the odd spontaneous Tuesday night or Saturday afternoon or something. (More on sex later.)

It's very good to have at least one night out a week together, because that breaks an over-domestic routine. But does it always have to be the same night? Do you always have to go to the same place or small selection of places?

Try to look at the elements of your routine and discuss it with your partner. Obviously you need some routine and structure in order to get done what needs to be done. But if you feel you could both benefit from a bit more flexibility and spontaneity, then do it.

2 Consider how to inject novel elements into your lives together. For example:

a Novel and unexpected expressions of love can be massively appreciated. Arranging a surprise romantic weekend; phoning unexpectedly during the day; that sort of thing. It may sound like something out of a soppy novel, but there *are* good psychological reasons for taking this sort of action.

b If you like eating out, explore different venues and styles of cooking and don't just stick with the tried and tested. If you like having dinner parties, try inviting some people you don't know very well but would like to know better. Invite friends in different combinations, so you don't always have Mike and Kate with James and Jo, triggering those endless conversations about tennis that you know bore you stiff. And you both might agree that you are, to be frank, getting a bit tired of that cottage in Norfolk for your main summer hols. Now, let's think, where else. . . .

c To spice things up, try a bit of secrecy. One study is rather intriguing in this respect. American psychologist Daniel Wegner and his colleagues gathered together groups of two men and two women to play cards. None of the players knew each other beforehand. Every group was divided into two competing pairs, each composed of a woman and a man seated opposite one another. In some groups, one of the couples was instructed to play with their feet touching under the table, and told that this was to be a secret from their opponents. In other groups, one pair had to touch feet but this did not have to be kept secret. The result? Afterwards, the couples who'd played secret footsie reported being more attracted to each other than the couples who'd touched openly.

Secrecy seems to form a strong social bond in general, the researchers say. This could be partly because of the mental effort needed not to give the secret away, which keeps you preoccupied with your partner. Secret affairs may be given a boost this way.

But if your current relationship is well known to all, what can you do? 'A few secret activities,' the researchers suggest, 'from weekends away from the kids to clandestine noontime trysts, might introduce a new dimension of excitement and awareness to the relationship.' And they'd certainly be a giggle.

d Are there activities that you know you both enjoy, but you rarely do because you don't get around to it/don't feel you can afford it? Let's say, for example, that you both love the theatre. That takes planning and money. OK, you might agree that you actually could afford to go roughly every six weeks. So one of you takes the responsibility for buying a listings magazine, initiating the discussion and making the booking. With luck you'll both have a really jolly evening that is out of the usual run.

The other person could take responsibility for organizing, say, a trip to the races or the seaside or an exhibition or wherever every few weeks.

e Are there activities that you or he enjoys, but the other person has never tried because they think they won't like it or can't do it? It might be worth one go, at least. You never know. . . .

f Are there things you or your partner has secret yearnings to try? If so, confess them. And ask him. He may have always wanted to go and watch mud wrestling, but never said so because he didn't think you'd enjoy it.

g Are there activities which neither of you has ever done, but you think you might both enjoy? Then give it a go. Developing new leisure activities together could be fun and form another binding element in your relationship. (Nothing's guaranteed, however – try to choose something that you do genuinely both enjoy and can both learn to do quite well. If he wants to be a knife thrower you might not fancy being a pincushion; and you don't want to be dangling from a rope at the summit of Mount Everest while he's still scrambling about on the foothills and suffering from vertigo.)

When you're thinking about activities that are brand-new to you both, try to be creative. You could even do some research – buy booklets that list local evening classes, for instance. You may both prefer classes on medieval English literature to an intense course of team skydiving.

But fresh, jolly activities that you enjoy doing together will stop you both slipping into the habit of seeing your partner as associated with nothing but the dull routines of life. 'Whose turn is it to wash the dishes? . . . I wish you wouldn't eat muesli – it welds to the bowl like ferret droppings. . . . Why do we always pick the check-out queue filled with people whose purchases have lost their blasted price labels . . .? You know washing that green T-shirt with my knickers makes them look bilious. . . . No, let's eat on our laps, it's that quiz show on telly. . . .'

In this atmosphere, it would hardly be surprising if your feelings of love and appreciation of the other person went into a complete coma.

Talking

Whatever activities you choose to do, it's very important to *talk* about them. It would be perfectly possible for you to go, say, to an art gallery and not to talk to each other.

But there's evidence that marital satisfaction is linked with spending leisure time together *plus* high levels of communication during it. 'Oooh, look, what a brilliant painting! Look at those jewel-like colours' and the reply 'Lovely. And you could almost eat the bread on that table,' is better than 'Pretty' 'Mnnngh.'

You could, of course, argue that leisure activities plus talking are linked with happiness because happy couples are more likely to spend time together and talk. This is, of course, true. But it is also very likely that doing fun things together *and talking about them* can boost marital happiness.

First, you associate the presence of your partner with feeling cheerful and having a good time. Second, talking is a way of maintaining and developing intimacy. That means talking not just about things done together, but about work and what's happened (no matter how apparently trivial) in the day. Such talking, according to British psychologist Dorothy Miell, enables couples to keep in touch with how each of them is looking at the world; to intertwine those views; and to monitor how they're both feeling and thinking.

It might help to choose activities which *are* a potentially rich source of things to talk about. Art galleries and museums, for instance, fall into that category. Tiddlywinks probably doesn't.

Talking can maintain, increase and elaborate your understanding of each other. Back in that art gallery – well, who knows . . .

You, gazing at a stuffed gerbil suspended in a glass tank of flat Lucozade: 'Good grief. The artist must think the British public has the IQ of an ant.'

Him: 'I know it might look like that, darling. But I think he's trying to say that in a world of flattened emotions, life is worth nothing.'

On second thoughts, divorce the idiot immediately.

No, no – seriously, you get the idea.

Doing interesting things also provides useful topics of conversation after the event. If they were intended to be fun and turned into a disaster for some reason, even that can be chewed over and laughed about once the immediate disappointment has passed.

It's important not to forget to keep talking when you're at home. Not constantly, of course, or you'd drive each other up the wall. But in one study, when men and women who were *happily* married were asked what changes they'd like in their spouse's behaviour, one of the top five requests of both sexes was that they wished the other would start interesting conversations.

It's quite easy to get lax in the conversational department. You feel secure and relaxed, you're tired, you're committed to the relationship – hell, you don't have to bother. The courting days of trying to be interesting seem long past.

Look back on the topics you've discussed with your partner over the last twenty-four hours. You may not actually have had more than fleeting conversations anyway. So how's it looking?

- who's going to give the dog his worm pill
- the drawer of your filing cabinet in the office has stuck
- his mother's just rung to say her knee's bad again
- your infant jolly nearly got his finger stuck in the plughole
- you're nearly out of loo paper

Gripping, huh?

Yes, these things do have to be talked about – not just for practical reasons, but because you need to keep communicating even about the trivial. But it would be nice to remember that your partner also has rather entertaining views on politicians, tells a good joke, or whatever. He may also need reminding that you're regarded as the group wit amongst your pals.

So try to get the old conversational ball rolling again if it's got stuck somewhere. Talk about things you've seen in the paper or on the TV, heard on the radio, gossip. Whatever. Ask him what he thinks about these things. Tell him straight that you love talking about things other than the current state of the drains, but that you seem to have got out of the habit, and please will he mention interesting topics too?

Even if he's always been a bit of a silent type, that doesn't mean he doesn't have thoughts about things. It would be nice to know what they were.

One type of event might encourage more interesting chats: evenings with friends.

Social events with friends

Spending time with friends can be fun, stimulating and enriching. It can also serve to shed new light on a partner (a good light, one hopes, though there are no guarantees in life!) How often has a friend asked your partner a particular question which you happen never to have asked, and you are intrigued and surprised by his response?

'Have you ever been down a coalmine, Phil?'

'Well, I did once, on a student trip. God, those guys earn their money. I remember. . . .'

Or you both feel jolted into making a conversational effort – and thus remind each other what good company you can be.

Try, though, to spend the majority of time with friends whom you *both* like. If he starts to associate you with evenings of boredom and annoyance, that will most definitely not be a good thing.

Occasionally, of course, evenings will have to be spent with friends of one of you that the other thinks are a bit of a bore. But you can negotiate this. 'Darling, in return for you spending a whole dinner party listening to Linda going on about her house renovation, I'll treat you to that new monster movie and buy you an enormous bucket of popcorn.'

It's also important to keep in mind that, although time spent with friends can be fun and enriching, you also need to have some happy and interesting times when it's just the two of you. One study found that those who did not spend much leisure time with the partner *on his or her own* were particularly dissatisfied with the quality and amount of time spent together.

So even if you feel tired and can't be bothered, if you make the effort to go out to do something enjoyable it can do your relationship good – and probably make you feel less tired too, I shouldn't wonder. . . .

Taking the partner's perspective

Attentiveness and thoughtfulness in a partner are, as we have seen, important elements in a relationship. To be attentive and thoughtful involves looking at things from his point of view – putting yourself in his shoes. The advantages of this are obvious.

1 It will enable you to judge what gestures might be appreciated. You know he's worried about that birthday coming up with a big '0' on the end. Knowing him as you do and putting yourself in his place, what would cheer him up the most? A vast surprise party? A small non-surprise dinner party? A trip to the theatre, just the two of you? A 'dirty' weekend in the country? Or something else? You might feel personally that the only way to celebrate a serious birthday is with a major bash. But when you think carefully about it from his point of view, you might decide that that will be the last thing *he* wants. Snogging on a *bâteau* on the Seine might bring him more pleasure.

2 When you need to communicate with him over something, it might help to put yourself in his place to judge how he

might react and therefore the best way to put it. This is especially important if it's something you are – or are about to be – in conflict over. One of the advantages of taking the partner's perspective is that you're less likely to go into personal attack mode. You'll see in advance how much that will upset or anger him and therefore what a useless strategy it is. You'll see how you'd feel if he turned to you and said what you were on the verge of saying to him – 'You bastard! How dare you invite your mother to stay for three weeks without consulting me.' Well, how would you feel?

Unfortunately, the sad news is that research finds women to be better at putting themselves in the other person's place than men are. In one study, by American researchers Edgar Long and David Andrews, members of married couples were asked two sets of questions.

1 People were asked to report on their own behaviour, such as:

– 'Before criticizing my partner I try to imagine how I would feel in his/her place.'
– 'I sometimes try to understand my partner better by imagining how things look from his/her perspective.'

2 Participants were asked how they saw their partner's behaviour. They had to rate the truth of statements such as:

– 'My partner is able to accurately compare his/her point of view with mine.'
– 'When my partner is upset with me he/she tries to put him/herself in my shoes for a while.'

The study showed that the more a person took their partner's perspective, the more satisfied with the relationship that partner was; and believing that the partner puts him or herself in one's own shoes was positively linked with one's own satisfaction. However, both sexes agreed that the women were better at perspective-taking than were their men; and a man showing competence in this area appeared to be particularly appreciated by the woman.

So as well as trying to look at things from your partner's viewpoint, you might have to encourage him to do the same for you. 'OK, imagine if you were me. How would you feel if by 9pm you'd heard no word from me and had no idea when I'd be home?'

Taking the other's perspective is something that can be learned. In the study I've just described, the couples had been married on average for about twenty-four years. Other evidence has suggested that, as time goes on, partners may make fewer and fewer efforts to keep tabs on the other person's feelings and state of mind because they have become over-confident. They feel they know almost everything there is to know. However, this is very risky. As we've just seen, trying to put yourself in your partner's shoes is a strategy related to happiness even after more than two decades.

A fair division of domestic chores

The fact is that, once you are both committed and living together, every morning you wake up to a welter of the practicalities of life. Who's going to get up first to put the kettle on and dole out the All-Bran? Possibly there are children to be sorted out (I'll discuss children in Chapter 5). Then there's probably paid work to be done by one or both of you; bulging plastic bags of shopping to be staggered home with; dishes to be washed; supper to be cooked or an evening out arranged; plus washing, loo cleaning, sewing on buttons, getting that nasty stain out of the carpet. Blind passion can come a severe cropper in arguments about who's going to tackle that stain.

In the 'equity' study I mentioned earlier, quite a few of the women were definitely feeling a sense of unfairness in the domestic chores department. It's not surprising – the evidence is that even women in full-time employment still retain major domestic responsibilities, whether or not they are parents. I've heard of a couple (now divorced) who would travel home from work together on the same train. But when they got in, he always settled into an armchair for the evening while she headed for a fun night in the kitchen.

Nor are there strong signs of vast improvement in the situation. A study of British teenagers published in 1989 found that far fewer boys than girls were doing their bit with the dustpan and spray polish. So many of the next generation of kids are being trained in the old ways.

If you have a man who thinks that the mere touch of a lavatory brush will deplete his testosterone, what can you do? (And no, you don't think his annual fiddle with the U-bend under the sink is a fair exchange.)

Using the communication skills already discussed, you need to be *assertive* – that is, to make your feelings known without attacking the other. Tell him calmly, clearly and explicitly.

This approach has a far greater chance of getting him to do what you want than a *passive* style, in which you don't express your feelings for fear of offending or disturbing him. Similarly, the assertive approach has a higher chance of success than the *aggressive* tactic, in which you let fly with attack and unconstructive criticism.

Let's see what these three approaches might look like. Say you want to persuade him to take an equal share in the house cleaning. At the moment, he washes the dishes and fits electric plugs with a flourish, but that's it.

Assertive

'Darling, I'm just feeling overwhelmed at the moment. I'm having to knock myself out at work on our new "Everyone can afford an oyster" campaign. Then I come home and have to do *everything* but the dishes – and I can't go on. We both work hard, but I feel we need to work out a way to share the domestic chores fairly. Can we sit down and list the chores, work out how often each needs to be done and how long they take, and then devise a system so that everything gets done and we spend equal time on them and take turns at things? So it's not always me squirting gunk into the lavatory bowl and sorting the whites from the coloureds? I know that this will mean some more work for you. But the pay-off will be that I'll be a lot less tired and ratty, which I expect you'd like! And also things will run much more smoothly. You won't be yelling "Where the hell are my lucky socks?" on your way to a vital meeting, when they're festering in the lowest and most ancient stratum of the laundry basket.'

In this speech, you have:

1 Been assertive about what you feel and what you think needs to happen.
2 Recognized *his* position – that he works hard too – while stating your own clearly.
3 Put forward a specific way of negotiating a fairer division of labour.
4 Incorporated a crucial ingredient of persuasion – shown how him doing what you want will benefit *him*.

Passive

'I'm so desperately busy at work. I feel so knackered when I get home. (Pause.) Oh well, I'd better nip down to the shops, peel the potatoes, grill the chops, clean the carrots, put on a wash, iron your shirts, have a go at that limescale on the bath and tackle that yukky blob on the rug. Like another cup of tea, darling?'

Forget it.

Aggressive

'You know how busy I am at work. It's hell trying to persuade people that something with the consistency of a slug and the taste of fish urine is worth paying inordinate amounts of money for. Then I come home and have to do every blasted thing while you sit around watching the football, you lazy, selfish toad. Either you start doing more about the house or one day you'll come home and I'll have changed the locks.'

Er – no. It *may* be temporarily effective in terms of spud peeling, but it will certainly be even more effective at corroding the marital atmosphere.

So get assertive. And tell him that of course there's one more benefit of a fair division of labour – it'll make more time for you both to go out and HAVE SOME FUN.

5

Crisis

Most couples in a long-standing relationship will face at least one major crisis. In this chapter I shall concentrate on two in particular – the arrival of a child (the little darlings can be a terrible shock to the system) and infidelity. But first, I want to make some general comments.

CRISES IN GENERAL

Sometimes a crisis occurs in the life of one of the partners – perhaps the loss of a job, or a bereavement. Sometimes the crisis affects both partners simultaneously, such as the loss of a person dear to you both. Or the accidental burning down of your house. Or. . . .

Such crises need not damage your relationship at all. But sometimes they do. What can you do to prevent this happening?

If the crisis affects one of you

One of the main risks here is that one partner fails to understand fully how the other is feeling. As a result, that partner becomes very intolerant of the other's behaviour. 'Why are you still so depressed? It happened *months* ago. . . .

Why won't you *talk* to me? . . . Now you're out of work, you could at least pick up the vacuum cleaner now and again, for God's sake.'

Obviously I can't address here all the possible crises which might arise. But what I can do is to make some general points.

If the crisis has happened to your partner

1 It is very important that you use the 'getting the other person to talk' and 'listening' skills already discussed. You'll find it all much easier to deal with if you can understand what's going on in his head. You will also help him a great deal by offering your empathy, understanding and support.

2 If you can, try to get hold of a book on whatever the crisis is. If you know that grief after bereavement may show particular features (such as preoccupation with the lost person) and that recovery may take some time, you will be prepared and, again, less intolerant.

   The same applies to, say, unemployment. Women often expect men who are unemployed to start doing far more in domestic tasks, and get extremely irritated if this doesn't happen. One reason it may not happen is that the man may be having a lot of trouble coming to terms with the loss of his job. He may strenuously resist having to redefine his identity as 'an unemployed man'. He may prefer to see himself as just very temporarily out of work. Therefore to undertake a major shift in the role he plays at home may seem like an admission of defeat, an acknowledgement of his new 'low-status' position in society. This is not an excuse for him not doing more about the house; but if something like this is going on in his mind it's better for you to know. Then you'll feel less cross, and you may be able to induce him to do more at home 'while he's searching for a new job'.

3 If your partner is clearly not even beginning to recover from the crisis and is, perhaps, still very distressed or

depressed some months after it has occurred, you might have to consider encouraging him to seek professional therapeutic help or counselling. Sometimes people can benefit from outside help to get over things. If it's bearing down on you and your relationship and you're nearing your tolerance limit, confessing this to your partner might spur him to go for the help he needs before you're both absolutely on the deck.

If the crisis has happened to you

1 Make sure that you explain fully to your partner how it has affected you, and keep him in periodic touch with developments. Over time your thoughts and feelings will shift, sometimes in unpredictable ways, and he will need to know what's going on. It will be hurtful and alienating for him to be kept at a distance from you during a difficult period in your life.
2 You too can try to get hold of a self-help book on your particular crisis. Go to a good bookshop, and ask friends and the bookseller for advice if you feel you can. Knowledge can help a lot when you are in pain.
3 As I've advised for your partner if he's the one in trouble, it may sometimes be that you need outside counselling as well. If the weeks are passing and you're not feeling any better at *all*, then getting help is something positive you can do. It's worth a try, for the sake of you and your partner – and your relationship.

If the crisis affects you both

The same three points apply.

1 Whatever you do, keep him informed of your feelings and persuade him to reveal his. Otherwise, there is a danger that you'll misinterpret each other's emotions and thoughts. People can have different ways of coping with crisis. Yours may be to stay indoors and cry a lot; his may be to get out

and play a lot of hard games of squash. You, however, might interpret this as evidence of callousness and insensitivity. You don't want to have any misunderstandings about what's going on here.

2 If there's a self-help book that looks useful and relevant, grab it.

3 If you're both really suffering and it's not getting better, then going for counselling together might be a step in the right direction.

Is the crisis controllable?

Some crises are not controllable: a bereavement, for example. It's happened, it's unalterable, and it's something that people need to come to terms with gradually, over time (see the three points above). There is evidence, too, that if the situation really is out of your control, what many people say about positive thinking is all true. Those who find something positive in awful, uncontrollable events show less distress than those who don't. This may be something quite abstract – such as changing or growing as a person because of what's happened.

But some crises may benefit from you and/or your partner taking action. In other words, these are events over which you *might* be able to exert some control.

Research on effective coping strategies is still at a relatively early stage. But there are indications that, on the whole, tackling the source of the problem is going to reduce the psychological damage of stressful events more than will trying to escape or evade the issue. What follows applies to you and/or your partner as appropriate.

Do

- Take action. Work out a plan of what to do to try to make things better Then do your best to follow this through, step by step. If it doesn't seem to be working, develop some new options.
- Seek social support. Talk to people about how you're feeling. It can help to tell others about your ghastly state – it's good to let it out somehow (about your sodden pillow, your insomnia, your fear that you'll never recover and so on), but don't *just* wallow in your negative emotions. It may make you feel even worse and hold you back from tackling the source of the problem. Ask others for positive input, too. Have they or anyone they know experienced anything similar, and if so, how did they feel and cope? If you respect their views, ask them for advice and, if it does indeed seem wise, follow it.
- Think positive. If there's anything at all positive to be found in the situation, emphasize that in your own mind. 'Yes, so I've lost my job. But at least I don't have to face that old tyrant Clampitt every morning and listen to him slurping his tea. It used to sound like my drains. And perhaps now I can try something a bit different . . .'

Don't

- Sit around having fantasies or wishes about how things might turn out.
- Daydream or imagine a better time or place than the one you are in.
- Wish that the situation would go away or somehow be over with.
- Think about fantastic or unreal things (such as helping an old man across the road and being left ten million quid) to make yourself feel better.
- Avoid being with people in general.
- Try to cheer yourself up by eating, drinking, smoking, using drugs or medication.

– Sleep more than usual.

This list of 'don'ts' might sound jolly tempting. But a research study by American psychologists Carolyn Aldwin and Tracey Revenson found that these 'escapist' strategies *increased* emotional distress after a stressful episode. The danger of such strategies may be that, although they might make you feel better temporarily, the cause of the stress is still lurking untouched and so the stress can build up. Some of the strategies, indeed, will in themselves probably make you feel worse again pretty quickly – such as being alone, or eating/drinking/smoking too much.

There is one stress that the majority of committed couples are going to have to face: the arrival of offspring.

CHILDREN

The arrival of a baby can be a great shock. Not the arrival as such, of course, but the impact on a couple's lives. It's very hard to imagine what it's *really* going to be like until it's happened.

The image of babies as binding a couple together with hoops of steel is a strong one. We often hear of couples who've had a baby in order to repair a faltering relationship. But that's not a good move. Producing offspring may mean that the relationship lasts longer than it otherwise would, because having children greatly raises the costs of ending it. But if the relationship is not working in itself, a child is unlikely to make it work – and it'll probably all collapse in the end.

A good or a bad impact?

One study looked at marriage a year after the birth of a first baby. Comparing satisfaction scores in early pregnancy with satisfaction when the baby was a year old:

- around 28 per cent showed a slight increase in satisfaction
- about 34 per cent showed no change or only a very small decrease
- around a quarter had a moderate fall
- just over one in ten had a substantial fall in marital satisfaction

So while the arrival of the baby did little or no marital harm for about 60 per cent, for two in five couples things were not so rosy. And about 40 per cent reported a damaging impact on their sex lives.

As the child starts to grow, things do not necessarily improve. The evidence is that, on average, marital happiness is lower when there are children living in the home. There's disagreement amongst researchers over whether – for those couples who've made it through and are still together – satisfaction rises again to what it was before the children arrived, or never makes it back to that level.

The crucial phrase here, of course, is 'on average'. This does not have to happen to you. But a good start to the process of protecting your marriage is to know the dangers beforehand.

Potential sources of trouble

The risk of marital trouble might come from several sources.

For him, who nearly always carries on working
- (initially) broken nights
- major changes in daily routines
- going out less
- a threesome (or more) in the home
- a shift in his wife's attention away from him
- decrease in time together as a couple
- possibly a lot of distressing and noisy crying

There is a lot for men to adjust to when the infant arrives – but the effects on women are even more far-reaching.

For her

- She may give up her job. This is a huge shift. If she loved the job, it's a serious loss. Even if she didn't, she's still lost adult companionship, a degree of independence, a life outside the home, money, a structure to her day.
- She will take on more housework than her partner, and the majority of the responsibility for childcare, whether she returns to work or not. Unfair as this is, the evidence is that this is what happens. You're clutching a J-cloth while he's clutching a whisky.
- Like the man, she will also have to face broken nights, huge changes in routines, going out less, having an extra human being around, less time with her partner, and possibly a lot of infant wailing.
- She may suffer post-natal depression.

Depression

Studies indicate that post-natal depression occurs in about 10–15 per cent of mothers; and milder depression may be reported by a further 16–20 per cent. Arguments still rage about the role of hormones and of psychological and social factors in these miserable feelings. But among the possible psychological and social factors which have been implicated, researchers have concluded that there's a lot of evidence for these three:

- a history of depression
- social adversity
- marital disharmony being already present before the child arrives.

There may be some dangers to your mental health a bit further down the line too. The idea that feminism is a bit passé seems to have been insidiously gaining ground for some time now. Waves of complacency have been induced by women's greater visibility in public life, stalking along in pencil skirts and swinging briefcases. But if everything is so wonderful for women these days, the findings of a 1991 British study are going to take a bit of explaining.

Jane Elliott and Felicia Huppert of Cambridge University analysed questionnaires filled in as part of the major nationwide Health and Lifestyle Survey by over a thousand British women who were under forty-five and married. The results revealed that 35 per cent of women with children aged between two and four were 'potential cases of psychiatric disorder'. Among women whose children were at school, the proportion showing signs of psychological disturbance dropped to 24 per cent – which still looks pretty sizeable to me.

Women who had toddlers and were out working full-time 'are particularly vulnerable to mental health problems', although the difference between them and the women who stayed at home wasn't large enough to be statistically significant.

If you are suffering from depression, I would seriously urge you to seek help. Your doctor should be able to refer you to a chartered clinical psychologist or professional counsellor to assist you through this rough patch. For your own sake, as well as any damage it might inflict on your partner, child and relationship, don't let it go on month after month.

Practical difficulties

So despite all the fine talk about women's 'advances' towards or even 'achievement' of equality, how much has changed? Many women isolated at home are suffering, and what help is there for mothers with jobs who don't have oodles of money to pay for nannies and cleaners to relieve the pressures?

In America, a study of dual-income families with children has looked at coping strategies and marital happiness. The strategy they found to be most strongly linked with marital satisfaction for women was 'reframing the problem'. The researchers, Elaine Anderson and Leigh Leslie, say: 'Reframing entails seeing a situation in a different way so that it no longer seems overwhelming or problematic to the family.'

For example, a mother having trouble finding good child-care might think it's because she's a poor organizer or 'no one's as good as the child's own mother'. Reframing might mean putting the difficulty down to the fact that 'quality childcare is simply very expensive and hard to find', and isn't to do with her ability as a parent.

Attributing the problem to external factors, not to short-comings in the couple themselves, should at least lessen personal blame and guilt. The researchers think the reason that a change of attitude seems beneficial is that there often isn't a great deal that parents can actually *do*. 'Factors such as flexible working hours, available/affordable childcare, care for sick children, and after-school care are all issues that employed parents struggle with but are often dictated by workplace, community, or government policy decisions.'

Back in Britain, Elliott and Huppert echo these senti-ments. 'If research on this subject is to have any real mean-ing or relevance for women, an understanding of the diffi-culty of fulfilling the dual roles of parent and paid worker in a society that provides minimal childcare facilities is necessary.'

Too right. And women at home shouldn't be forgotten, either. Anyone who thinks that we can all relax with a satisfied smirk at our achievements is due for a harsh awakening.

Where is the 'new man'?

Regrettably, the new, reconstructed man has still very definitely not arrived.

Why, you ask, are women not asking for more help? Another British study, by social psychologists Rosaleen Croghan and Dorothy Miell – mainly of women who didn't have full-time jobs outside the home – found several reasons for these women's reticence. They believed the responsibility for parenthood rested with them, and so they didn't believe they had the right to demand equity or equality of input from the man. They also wanted to maintain the belief that their relationship was fine, and as long as they got emotional support from him they were willing to accept 'a marked degree of inequality'. So they would talk about how busy their husband is, how they need the money that he brings in by working so hard, how his work is more important than theirs. They'd also say he was slower at noticing things that were wrong with the child, couldn't initiate, was incapable. They wanted to explain what was happening in terms of external factors, not in terms of the active choices made by their partner and the power structure of the relationship itself.

But the women still had to face serious inequity on a day-to-day basis. Yet because to be angry was 'illegitimate', and they felt very uncertain about what it *was* fair to expect, they often felt guilty about raising the question of him increasing his share of the domestic work and childcare. They were also easily defeated if he didn't want to cooperate.

If the woman works, then it's likely that the man will do a bit more – but still less than the woman. And even this increased effort doesn't mean that all is rosy. In an American study of middle-class couples, the more husbands did around the home and children, the more resentful they felt and the more guilty the wives felt. This was true even though the wives were doing far more than their husbands, whether the wives worked or not. Close encounters with a mop, it seems, can make a man come over all peculiar.

So even when the women are working, the notion that they must be primarily responsible for home and children is still doing its insidious, deadly work. Indeed, women may sometimes be actively doing themselves a disservice here. There's some evidence that in families where fathers had the main responsibility for childcare for a significant chunk of the week, the women seemed rather threatened – they became resentful of him taking over family responsibilities, irritated by his standards of childcare and so on.

I have painted a grim picture because there's no point in closing our eyes to what is happening. Every woman is going to have to make her own judgements and conduct her own negotiations about how things are to be organized after the arrival of children. But it is clear from all this research that many women are, for reasons of their own, sacrificing themselves to an unnecessary degree. As a result, their relationship could suffer if this leads to a build-up of anger and resentment. Any such negative feelings may also be fighting an exhausting internal battle with the thoughts which run 'You have no right to feel like that – he's a wonderful husband and father, and he plays with the children every Sunday.'

What can you do?

So what action can you take?

Organizing time

Think hard about how you *do* want your lives together to be organized. Think about it in detail.

- If you and your partner both do paid work, how many hours do you each spend on that work?
- What domestic jobs need to be done every week about the house, and how long do they take?
- Do you both have a roughly equal number of hours in the week when you and he are *not* doing paid work or housework or practical childcare jobs? Is it possible to organize that?
- During the part of the day when you are both at home is there an equal division of playing with child/nappy changing/feeding/bathing/calming down and other domestic duties?

The way you restructure your lives together *must be negotiated between you*. You must discuss the division of housework. You must discuss the division of childcare. You must discuss how to make sure you have some fun and relaxation. You must try to work out what's fair.

You need to agree plans between you. Then you need to check how they're working – say, every month. You need to check not just how they're working in a practical sense – 'But I thought *you'd* cleaned her teeth' – but how you're both feeling about it. If either of you is, say, resentful or guilty or both, then talk about it. It may be that, over time, airing the issue will induce a shift in the way you and/or he are thinking about things, and that this will rectify any negative feelings; or you may need to revise the plans somewhat.

This will be better than saying nothing, but feeling all resentful because here we are in the nineties, and his contribution is a bit of superficial New Mannishness: the occasional nappy change, half an hour of helping little Damian construct laser guns out of Lego, and that's about it. There's evidence that even in relationships that are pretty egalitarian before children come along, after the arrival of the little bundle there is often a shift towards a more 'traditional' male–female division of labour in the home.

So talk to him. And if you're lucky enough to have any spare money, you might want to consider using it to ease the burden.

Remembering love

As well as the practical aspects, don't neglect the emotional ones. Researchers observing new parents at home found them to be less involved with one another and to show less affection than during the pregnancy.

It is unwise to divert all attention away from the partner and towards the baby/infant/young child (obviously as children grow this will happen less and less as they develop their own lives, but you don't want harm to have been done by then).

To show love and affection – even if it's just a kiss as you wipe the sick off his jumper while he clutches the baby – won't take hours of time or kilojoules of psychological and physical energy. Yet it can help to keep the two of you together *as a couple*, not flung into the roles of 'co-parent' to the neglect of your central bond.

Having fun

Make sure, whatever you do, that you have some fun:

1 With the child or children – going on a picnic, to a fair, whatever you fancy.
2 Just the two of you. Try to find a small number of people who can babysit, and for goodness' sake try to have an evening out once a week (more – if you want to, of course – as the child grows). You don't want to become so overwhelmed by the demands of child-rearing that you spend no happy times alone as a couple.

Obviously your children can be enormous fun, and are wonderful and beloved and thrilling. I have dwelt on the negative aspects of their presence because, of course, there lie the risks. Having fun with your child is great and should be a binding element in your relationship. But you also need some grown-up fun, I believe, where your partner is the focus of the event. You need to have a good time with *him*, and him with you. You don't want to be having a good time just because little Max is being entertaining. In essence, you would be:

1 Reminding yourself afresh of why you love this person (and vice versa).
2 Associating happy feelings with being in their company (not, as I've said, just images of sprout-peeling and other such mundane and boring matters).

You musn't assume that you can put your relationship on

the back burner for a while. In my view, this is an extremely dangerous assumption. A damaging space might develop between you that can be hard to bridge. Don't take the risk.

Sex

You may need to be a bit creative in terms of your sex lives for a while. Often it's difficult at first, perhaps for physical reasons (intercourse may be painful, say, as a result of an episiotomy) and exhaustion. However, your partner is having to come to terms with a certain diversion of your attention away from him. If you can manage not to compound this by making him feel physically undesirable as well, this might help.

I am *not* suggesting you force your exhausted frame into endless sexual marathons. But there's a great deal to be said for making him realize that you still love him even if for a while you can't manage things quite as before. Even if you don't yet feel able to have full sex (there's evidence that nearly all women will have resumed intercourse by the twelfth week after the birth, and around a third to a half by six to seven weeks), you can still indulge in some fulfilling sexual activity.

Try not to permit the total – or near-total – collapse of your sex life. I know this can be tricky with babies and children around. All I can say is that it's an area to watch out for and in which to be as creative as you can within the limits of practical possibilities.

For instance, perhaps you could recruit allies. Could you set up a reciprocal deal with, say, two couples who are close friends who have children roughly the same age as yours? One night in the week, you each have the children of the other couples round to your place. How long this would be for would depend on the children's ages, of course. But even if they're young and have to go to bed early, a couple of hours absolutely to yourselves could be a window of opportunity to do whatever you both feel like doing.

So in return for one evening (or part-evening) of probable

hell, you could have two periods of absolute aloneness together to refresh your relationship in whatever way you choose. But that's just a thought, and may be absolutely useless for you.

If it *is* useless for you, why not think: 'Well, that won't work, but come to think of it, what we could do is. . . .'

Idiosyncratic solutions

I realize that it's all very well to talk 'in theory' about ways of not letting the process of child-rearing damage your marriage. The point is simply that there is – unfortunately – no question that having children *can* rock the boat, and you need to pre-empt as many problems as possible.

Each couple will come up with their own particular solutions. There are, after all, a great variety of ways in which you can organize your lives together once your offspring have arrived, and which would help to keep your relationship on track. The precise day-to-day details only you and your partner can work out.

But with some vigilance on your part, I hope you can hugely relish the joys of parenthood, cope with its stresses and anxieties – and survive with your relationship intact. Indeed, it may even be strengthened in the process.

INFIDELITY

Studies show that infidelity is one of the most upsetting things for either sex to have to deal with in a relationship. It can trigger great hurt, jealousy and a strong sense of rejection, and seriously devastate feelings of trust in the other person.

If your partner has been unfaithful

There's evidence that he is more likely to tell you than you are accidentally to discover tell-tale hotel bills. The immediate question is – why did he do it? The main causes of infidelity that have been identified are:

- dissatisfaction with the marriage (or committed relationship)
- sexual dissatisfaction
- wanting sexual variety/experimentation
- excitement
- revenge against the partner/anger/jealousy
- ego bolstering

A few couples may have agreed between them that infidelity is acceptable; but for most people this is not the case. If your partner has been unfaithful, it's vital to find out why. It could also help to know the nature of the unfaithfulness. After all, the term covers a wide variety of actions. It can include, for instance, a one-night stand that is your partner's only infidelity ever; a series of flings recently; a long series of flings beginning shortly after you were married; a long-standing and loving relationship, which he would have moved into if it weren't for the children. The causes of one-off infidelity and/or recent infidelity may be more easily dealt with than those of chronic and incorrigible unfaithfulness or a serious and long-standing extramarital love affair.

But only some serious talking is going to reveal what those causes are and therefore what the potential remedies might be.

Dissatisfaction with the marriage

Contrary to the stereotyped belief, sexual dissatisfaction with one's spouse is not always the main cause of sexual straying, for men or for women. Indeed, there's evidence that the unfaithful often emphasize other aspects of their extramarital relationship – such as feeling loved and wanted, self-discovery and talk.

So if the motive was that he was dissatisfied with your relationship, the question then becomes: is whatever he was dissatisfied with rectifiable or not? For instance, if he has been feeling neglected because of your preoccupation with work/children, that is alterable – negotiating shifts in priorities, changes in the practical ways you live your lives, and so on.

But perhaps, say, you have both changed a great deal during the years of your marriage. Perhaps you have, for various reasons, not kept each other involved with and in touch with those changes. 'Darling, I want to stop being a supermarket cashier and train to be an estate agent. Just let me tell you what my average day is like right now, and perhaps you'll understand. . . .'

Perhaps the more dependent, domestic woman he married has become increasingly independent and is in a flourishing career – and this is something that he does not want at all. Extremely fundamental issues like this may be very hard to negotiate. I mean, do you want to carry on spending your days waiting in for the washing machine repairer – or grab your briefcase and head for the office? Is what it would take to rectify your relationship in his eyes actually too great a sacrifice to make? Maybe he can be persuaded that you can still give him all the things he truly needs – love, sex, companionship – even though you're a career woman. It's just that he might have to iron his own shirts.

Whether or not the root causes of his dissatisfaction with your marriage are mendable can only be worked out when you know what the hell they are. The communication skills we looked at earlier should help you to winkle them out of him.

It may be, of course, that he now feels so estranged from you that he has told you of his infidelity as he is packing his suitcase, leaving you to pick up the psychological pieces. (I shall examine this process in a later chapter.)

But if this is not the case, then I believe that ferreting out the truth is crucial, whichever way your relationship finally goes. If it is to have a chance of surviving, you can't move forward without a thorough understanding of what he is unhappy about in order to give you both the best chance of working on it. Even if, sadly, you decide in the end to part, it is far better to know exactly what went wrong. This gives you a chance of not falling into the trap of thinking,

'Oh, my relationships always go wrong. Men are bastards!' With a specific understanding of what went wrong in this relationship, you won't start generalizing to all future relationships and to all members of the opposite sex. Also, if there are any lessons to be learned, you can learn them. If the worst happens and he tells you how unhappy he is as he's literally heading for the front door, still try to get him to tell you later what the problem was. However difficult it is to hear, it's better to know.

Motives other than marital dissatisfaction

Again, you can't move forward unless you know what they are.

- If it's sexual dissatisfaction, then what is it? He wants more sex? He wants more experimental sex? He wants you to be more enthusiastic? He wants you to initiate sex? He wants you to spurn his advances with the 'I'm too tired' plea less often? What?

When you've got a clear picture, You can think about what you want to do.

- If it's sexual variety or experimentation, of what nature? In other words, is he sick of the missionary position on Saturdays with the light off, or is it that he wants different women, not different positions?

If he's sick of the m.p. on Saturdays, that can be changed pretty easily.

If he wants different women for sexual variety, that presents much more of a problem. This is something that comes from within him, and is not to do with you. If this is his prime motive, then it's very likely that he has had quite a number of affairs, even if you have only recently found out. This is a tricky one, and you may need some outside assistance. If he is sufficiently motivated to keep the marriage going, he may agree to go for counselling to explore why he feels the need to act in this way.

And he may well wish to stay married to you. It's very possible that in his mind he feels he loves you, and that these other flings are 'meaningless'. Research has found that men are more likely than women to have had extramarital sex without emotional involvement. Nevertheless, this may be pretty cold comfort for you. But if you want to keep his emotional involvement and not be miserable, he needs to crack this upsetting habit.

One further possibility here is that he doesn't regard extra-marital sex as a threat to your marriage. If so, this needs to be discussed – and, ideally, should have been made clear at the beginning. One study of British women and men (who had agreed to take part in research on adultery, and may not be totally representative) found less infidelity when both partners were clear that they were expected to be faithful than when the matter had not been discussed and was somewhat ambiguous. So get it straight early on if you can.

– If he has had an affair for excitement, then you need to know if this is because – even though he still loves you – your life together has become dull and routine, and thus his emotions have become deadened. If that's it, then start livening things up – as we saw earlier. Exciting holidays, taking up potholing, breeding lizards, whatever.

If he seeks 'excitement' because infidelity is his way of dealing with internal problems, then again he may need professional help to sort out whatever those problems are. You and he as a couple may not be able to do it alone.

– If it's revenge against you, or anger with you, or jealousy – why is this? Have you been having an affair? Does he think you're having an affair? Is he angry with you because he feels you've been neglecting him?

If you've been having an affair, this is very serious, as we will see shortly.

If he is chronically jealous but has no cause, then again you may need to persuade him to seek some therapeutic help. Chronic and unnecessary jealousy is likely to stem from a very low sense of self-worth. You may find that, however much you tell him you love him and he has no need to be jealous, he doesn't believe you. If nothing you say makes any difference, he may just have to talk to an outsider about it.

– If he's had an affair because he needs his ego boosting, this could be for a variety of reasons. Perhaps you've been together so long that you've forgotten to do it; perhaps he's feeling very undermined at work and has had his self-esteem eroded; perhaps he's having a mid-life crisis; perhaps he's looked in the mirror and seen the first grey hair in his eyebrows. You could try a bit of creative thinking: dragging him into bed more often, discussing job changes – anything that might make him feel better about himself.

If you feel able to reaffirm your love for him, and he still loves you, you may be able to talk it through and weather the storm. I say 'if you feel able to reaffirm your love' because you may not be able to. You may never be able to again – or you may be able to in a while.

But even if you do still love him, this does not mean that you should be frightfully and insincerely nice and understanding from the moment of revelation. It's important for you to express your feelings of anger, hurt, pain and jealousy. I know I've said that it's important to say 'I feel angry . . .' rather than 'You vile bastard'. If you need to say the latter in this moment of great extremity – well, then you will. But if you want to repair things, try as far as you can to focus on *telling* him all your feelings, rather than attacking so viciously (and over such a long period of time) that it may be even harder for the relationship to recover. Because it's important that you have your say. If you're to have a chance to get back on track, I don't believe this should be done by hiding your true feelings. All that will do is estrange you further from him in your heart of hearts, and sow the seed for a very acidic build-up of resentment. Instead of getting it all off your chest, you may let it out in endless drips of snide comments, sharp remarks and so on that will make the home a living hell for you both.

So get your feelings out. Get him to talk. If you can manage to accept that your partner is not perfect, understand the reasons the infidelity has happened and take steps to deal with them, this might help restore to you a feeling of power and control, as well as minimize the chances of it recurring.

If you are to get over your hurt and come to trust him again, he will also need to make strong attempts to reassure you of his love.

If it's not too late for either or both of you, emotionally speaking, you've got a chance of coming through this. To illustrate: one study of ways of dealing with a partner's infidelity found that being maritally satisfied was linked with a problem-solving approach to resolving the conflict that had arisen. Other approaches – avoiding the issue, being soothing, being aggressive, compromising – were all linked with dissatis-faction. But when two things are linked, it doesn't show what is causing what. It may be that initially strong marriages are the ones most likely to use the conflict-resolution tech-nique that has the greatest chance of success. Or it may be that problem-solving can help to restore the marriage.

Probably both are true. There is certainly some evidence that those who stay together after infidelity report being significantly more satisfied with their main relationship than do those who split up after such a crisis and form new relationships.

If you've been unfaithful

If you have been – or are being – unfaithful, you are one of an apparently growing band of women. It's very hard to do accurate surveys on sexual matters. Is the sample representative of the population as a whole? Are people telling the truth? However, what evidence there is suggests that, although in the past more men were adulterous than women, the numbers of women who are unfaithful are now catching up with the men. Two British surveys carried out in the 1980s, for example, found that just over a quarter of both men and women admitted to extramarital sex.

But the precise percentages do not, I believe, matter much. The point is that it happens, and not that infrequently. And even if the numbers of unfaithful women are growing, the evidence is that there are still sex differences.

Analysing your motives

The evidence suggests that a woman is more likely than a man to be unfaithful because she is unhappy with her marriage. Women seem more influenced than men by the risks of adultery, and believe they are more likely to occur – the risks of the marriage splitting up if they are discovered (and a greater chance of relative poverty as a result, never mind the struggles of single parenthood), of guilt, of pregnancy. So to run such risks, many women may need to be very highly motivated. Indeed, women who are unfaithful tend to have fewer adulterous liaisons than do unfaithful men. One study found that women involved in extramarital affairs were more likely than similarly involved men to say that falling in love justified such relationships; the involved men were more likely than the women to say that sexual excitement did.

So if you are being or have been unfaithful, this may be for any of the reasons listed at the beginning of this section. But the most likely one for you is that you are cheesed off with your marriage.

In an ideal world, if you are tempted to be unfaithful, you need to sit down and think *why* you want to do it *before* you take any action. Is it that he's been making you feel you have the sex appeal of a hearthrug? Do you have a closer relationship with your best saucepan than you do with him?

In this ideal scenario, you work out what's wrong and talk it through with your partner, and try to see if what's wrong can be made right. If it can, the temptation should be greatly lessened (even if you still find your partner's potential rival attractive) because the motivation has had its legs chopped from under it.

If the temptation has made you try to sort things with your partner, yet you have both – despite your best efforts – failed, then at least you might have a less messy and painful break than you would if you entered an extramarital affair and expressed your displeasure that way.

However, the ideal scenario does not always occur. Indeed, it is sometimes the extramarital relationship itself that clarifies feelings about the main relationship, be they good or bad. So if you are in an affair which is still going on, or have had an affair, you still need to do some hard thinking about why it has happened. If you have some core problems with your marriage, this won't solve them. If you believe your marriage is fine, and you are doing this – or have done this – for fun/excitement/flattery only, then I'd say:

1 Are you absolutely sure that that's all it is? That you're not harbouring discontents about your main relationship which you haven't faced up to?
2 If you feel certain that's all it is, and that the 'adventure' is harmless and won't damage your marriage, I wouldn't be too sanguine about this.

What damage might it do?

Unfaithful partners have been known to report that the extramarital relationship benefits – or is not harming – their marriage. This may sometimes be true. However, psychologists now think that such statements are often likely to be either a rationalization of what the person is doing, or else the result of failing to see what is actually happening to the marriage. It is very likely, it seems to me, that the possession of such a major secret will distance you from your partner.

There'll be no chance at all of being sanguine if your partner finds out that you are being – or have been – unfaithful.

Finding out that your spouse has been having an affair is lacerating, whichever sex you are. But one research study has looked at whether or not the sexes differ in any way in how they react. And is it worse if the rival is unattractive? Or if the affair is committed?

Two Israeli psychologists, Arie Nadler and Iris Dotan, gave over a hundred married people, aged between twenty-seven and forty-five, a story vignette. In the story, a friend rang the hero or heroine and revealed that the latter's spouse was romantically involved with somebody else.

The stories varied in a couple of respects (respondents each got a story where the protagonist was the same sex as they were): the rival was described as being either a physically attractive, successful professional or a short, fat junior sales-person in a large shoe store. (The participants themselves were middle- and upper middle-class.) Also, the friend with the big mouth said either that the rival had been seeing the protagonist's wife/husband for about a year and they seemed very involved; or that it appeared to be an uncommitted, one-time affair.

When asked how they thought the protagonist would feel and react, the 'type' of infidelity did seem to matter. For both men and women the worst situation was when the spouse was highly committed to an attractive rival. Here, what are threatened are both the protagonist's self-esteem (by the rival's attractiveness) and the marriage itself (because of the spouse's commitment). Commitment to an unattractive rival, however, was not seen to be quite so devastating – at first sight surprising. 'If my spouse prefers *that* to me. . . .' But the researchers think this is because, if the rival isn't such a big deal, it doesn't set up all sorts of negative comparisons to oneself, and the affair may be seen as unlikely to last even if one has been told that the spouse is relatively committed.

However, the sexes differed in the way they reckoned the protagonist would behave. The women were more likely to say that she would attempt to mend the marriage; the men tended to believe that the man would distance himself from it – start dating other women or getting a divorce. Indeed, the male respondents who said they were personally prone to jealousy were particularly likely to say that the man would withdraw.

Overall the men, the researchers say, 'appeared to be driven by their concern with protecting their egos; females, on the other hand, seemed most concerned with protecting their relationships'.

The idea that relationships are more at risk when it's the woman who is unfaithful is supported by British and American research, too. The old double standard, where men's sexual straying is more tolerated than women's, still hasn't lain down and died: 'Oh God, men!' 'How bloody dare she?'

So if the boot's on the other foot, you may be busily trying to get to the root of things – as in the previous section. But if you're the strayer, he's more likely to say, 'To hell with you' and go off in a huff.

Facing the risks you are running may help you to examine your own true feelings about your central relationship. Then you need to decide what to do.

If you want to stay in your marriage

If your partner doesn't know what you've done, and you want to stay in the marriage if certain things change, then those certain things need to be discussed with him. The events that triggered your re-examination – falling for another man – are not relevant. It's your main relationship that is the focus.

If you feel you want to end the marriage, all I'd say is be *very sure* that (a) it is not saveable and (b) you are leaving *because* it is not saveable, not just because you've found someone else. Although one hopes the next relationship would work out happily long-term, there are no certainties. So you need to be able to say to yourself – *if* it doesn't work out with my new man, I'm not going to wish I'd stayed with my husband.

If your partner does know what you've done, and you wish to save your marriage, then you will need to put in a major effort. What you need to do for him is what you hope he'd do for you if he was the one who'd been unfaithful.

– Apologise. Don't try to shirk responsibility by making excuses ('The conference hotel had such a romantic atmosphere – you could barely see the speakers for potted palms'). Don't try to justify why you were attracted to your lover ('It was just that he kept sweeping me off for hugely expensive dinners. I was constantly eating caviar and being blinded by the candlelight glinting off his Rolex').

Excuses and justifications might be taken to indicate that you're just weak and vulnerable to temptation and outside circumstances. This will be very alarming for your partner, as it implies that you could quite easily be knocked off the straight and narrow again in the future. Apologising shows that you are taking responsibility for what you have done, that you are truly sorry, and carries the implication that – provided you can sort things out – there is no reason for it to happen again.
– Reassure him that it is him you truly love.
– Tell him truthfully why you did it. Then you can both take action to address those reasons, by which means he can gradually be reassured that, since you've (let's hope) dealt with whatever the problem(s) was or were, he need not fear that you will do it again.

There is no doubt that infidelity can trigger the end of a relationship. But as we have seen, sometimes it would be a great shame if it did, and such an outcome is not inevitable. But if you want to keep your main relationship together, you're going to have to do some psychological white-water rafting for a while.

6

Sex

It's a bit difficult to think about a heterosexual relationship without thinking about the sex. It would be like strawberry bombe without the strawberries, really. It's a topic of perennial fascination – and it's complex. But here goes.

IN THE BEGINNING

In the 1990s, the question 'Shall we have sex?' is going to be raised pretty early in a budding relationship. One study published in the early 1980s found that, on average, men didn't 'expect' sex until roughly the fifth date. Of course, the AIDS fear has become very prominent since then; but the point is that the issue will often be raised very early – sometimes even on the first date.

Men's vs. women's attitudes to sex

The trouble is that, even as we approach the end of the twentieth century, there are still differences between men's and women's attitudes to sex. Research indicates that men are still – on average – more permissive than women. In one American study by psychologists Susan Hendrick and Clyde Hendrick and their colleagues, for instance, the men agreed but the women disagreed with statements such as: 'I do not need to be committed to a person to have sex with him/her'; 'Casual sex is acceptable'; 'I would like to have sex with many partners'; 'One-night stands are sometimes very enjoyable'; 'Sex as a simple exchange of favours is OK if both people agree to it.'

The men were fairly neutral about – but the women disagreed with – statements such as: 'It is OK to have ongoing sexual relationships with more than one person at a time'; 'It is possible to enjoy sex with a person and not like that person very much'; 'Sex is best when people approach it as good physical release.'

The men were again fairly neutral, while the women agreed, that 'To have good sex, two people have to know each other pretty well' and 'Sex without love is meaningless.'

The reason for pointing out that these are *average* sex differences is, of course, because some women are permissive and some men are not. But what these findings point to is a potential risk in the early stages – that you interpret his hot sexual passion for you as being more *emotionally* significant than it actually is. The fact that he lusts after you says nothing in itself about the strength of his affection – it may do, of course, but it may not.

The risk of misunderstanding the emotions that lie behind his passion is higher the earlier in the relationship you have sex. Obviously, if you don't make love until some way into the relationship, you'll have a much better idea of what's really going on here.

If you want to have sex with him for the sake of it, that's one thing. But if you want sex as part of – as you see it – a burgeoning relationship, it is wise to be sure that's what he wants too. Otherwise you might wake up after your first-date-night-of-passion looking forward to a blossoming romance while he leaves after the cornflakes, never to be seen again.

Painful.

Of course, if sex and emotion are more likely to be entwined for a woman, and less so for a man, this doesn't mean that sex and emotion aren't frequently combined for a man.

Indeed, this can lead to a potentially embarrassing misunderstanding in the early stages of some relationships.

A reluctant male

We're always hearing that men are such rampant sexual creatures – always on for it, any time, anywhere, with anyone. However, a Canadian study has looked at a rarely discussed aspect of male–female relationships; those occasions on which a woman wants sex and her partner doesn't.

This turns out, surprisingly for the stereotype, to be a common event. Two psychologists, Lucia O'Sullivan and Sandra Byers, gave questionnaires to about 180 male and female students who weren't dating each other. About half the women (49 per cent) said they'd had such a disagreement about sexual activity – most often intercourse – on a date in the past year alone; and 64 per cent of the men.

The men were most likely to attribute their reluctance to internal reasons: their feelings about the inappropriateness of the relationship (45 per cent) or that the timing in the relationship was wrong (21 per cent). ('Physical reasons' came third; it seems that only about one in six men really do have a headache.)

The women, in contrast, thought male reluctance was more to do with external factors, such as it being the wrong time or place. Only a small minority admitted it was something to do with the appropriateness or timing of the relationship. That, after all, has more worrying implications for the state of emotional play – at that point in the game, at least.

Once turned down, just over half the women said they complied without trying to persuade him; one in ten said they didn't comply (and tried to engage in the sexual activity regardless, or got heavy in some way); 38 per cent said they complied with the man's wishes but tried to get him to change his mind. The women's top six seduction strategies were:

- flirted
- touched or stroked him

- complimented him on his body or sexuality
- made positive comments about his appearance
- tickled him
- pouted or sulked (these last being usually received badly by the man)

On the whole, these strategies didn't work. Two-thirds of the women said the man didn't do what they wanted (on that date anyway); one in five got their own way later in the date; only one in ten won him over at the time.

There were costs involved, though. Women who reported trying to use influence remembered the encounter as less pleasant than did those who had merely complied with the man's refusal. This could explain, the researchers say, 'why women are somewhat reluctant to use influence'.

So to the many women whose men have turned them down and who have never liked to admit it, take heart. You're very far from being alone. And, remembering that sex differences are only averages, perhaps it's time to change the image of male sexuality from universally wanton and unquenchable to often sensitive and emotional. . . . It would probably come as a great relief to them.

And now we come to another major issue to be dealt with at the beginning of a sexual relationship.

Protection against AIDS

Since I am neither an AIDS expert nor a medical doctor, I am not going to list preventative measures here. If you are sexually active, these days it is obviously essential to keep track (via the media, public information leaflets and so on) of current thinking on 'safer' practices. Apart from obvious things such as cutting down on the number of partners you have, one of the messages constantly dinned in by the media is always to use a condom. Using condoms as an example, I want to look at some of the psychological factors which might intervene to prevent you confronting the problem.

One factor is your own and your partner's perception of the risk. The trouble here is not only that human beings are rather poor at assessing risks, but that you might mistakenly believe that you can 'tell' if someone is a risk (you can't) and that you can judge from what they tell you about their sexual history and any drug abuse how much of a risk they are. But you can't.

First, they might not be telling you the whole truth. Second, even the person themselves can't be 100 per cent certain – even if they've slept with only a few people, how can they be sure of those people's histories?

The third problem with assessing risk is that there's evidence that men see the risk of becoming infected as much lower than women do. The trouble is that it's men who have to wear the condoms, and so they may be very resistant. They may say there's no risk, they 'hate condoms', condoms feel like plastic bin bags, and so on.

So – you've met a new man. You want to make love. You, a sensible woman, want him to use a condom. If he is happy with that – no problem. But what if he isn't?

It might help if you're prepared for the strategies he's most likely to use to persuade you into condomless sex. A study of American students, by Sherrine Chapman De Bro and her colleagues, has uncovered the men's top three such tactics.

1 *Seduction.* To try to get the women really excited sexually and begin making love without a condom (the most popular method).
2 *Risk information.* Statements it would be unwise to rely on, such as: 'I would inform her that there have been very few cases of AIDS among heterosexual college students, so there is no need to use a condom.'
3 *Reward.* 'I would stress how very happy and pleased I would be with her for not insisting on the use of a condom.'

The men reported rarely using emotional coercion (the 'If you pressure me, then you mustn't care about me very much' tactic); deception (such as hiding the condoms); or saying they would make love *only* without a condom.

A great start when it comes to resisting unfair attempts at influence is to recognize what they are. So what, in your turn, can you do to persuade your new man into a condom? The researchers asked the women in their sample how effective they thought such strategies would be for getting him to use one. The three strategies these women rated highest were:

1 *Withhold sex.* You say you'll make love only *with* a condom. (The women rated this as likely to be the most effective strategy, and also the one they would feel most comfortable using.)
2 *Risk information.* You tell him that it *is* risky to have unprotected sex.
3 *Deception.* You don't say you want him to wear a condom because of the risk of sexually transmitted diseases; you tell him that it's pregnancy you're worried about.

Offering him rewards (telling him, say, that his respect for your feelings would really enhance your relationship) was seen as probably somewhat less effective, and emotional coercion (focusing on your displeasure if he doesn't do what you want) and seduction (rather difficult as he's the one who's got to wear the condom) pretty ineffective.

You can always try several strategies, of course. And if he still insists on unprotected sex – well, what are doors for? After all, seeing his reaction to your extraordinarily sensible request can be very revealing of what he is like as a person. If his response is immature, inconsiderate, selfish, blackmailing, irresponsible and bullying – well, this may make your decision about whether or not to pursue this relationship pretty easy.

Don't get paralysed by thoughts such as: 'Oh, I can't discuss this, I'm too embarrassed'; or 'What'll he think of me if I produce a condom?'; or 'It'll spoil the atmosphere.'

- If you have to weigh up a twinge of embarrassment against a chance of becoming infected with HIV, it seems terribly obvious which should win.
- You might (wisely) have already got some condoms yourself. Don't worry that he might think you sleep with millions of men when you don't. It would be very immature of him to think so, and it's contradictory and sexist to expect women to have sex and yet not be prepared for it.
- Don't fret about 'spoiling the romantic spontaneity' of it all – again, a feeble consideration when set against the possible consequences of not protecting yourself. And don't forget that correctly used condoms are extremely useful in protecting against other sexually transmitted diseases too.
- If you can't *talk* to him about protection, are you sure you *do* want to have sex with him? There's no doubt that many people do find these matters hard to discuss. It does seem extraordinary, when you think of it, that the physical act of making love can seem less intimate than actually talking about it.

   But these days, talking is vital. To minimize any emotional heat, you could always introduce the topic impersonally – 'I saw this article the other day about how important it is to use condoms' – just to get the issue aired. Or simply be very matter-of-fact – the 'if you haven't got any I have' approach. You can talk about protecting *both* of you, to minimize the chances of him being 'offended' at the mere notion that he might have a sexually transmittable disease or the 'if you loved me you'd trust me' line – both immature reactions in any case. And though many men – and some women too, of course – say they 'don't like condoms', in fact with condoms these days little or no sensation is lost, and believing otherwise is no reason not to give them a serious try. What's more, with practice they become easy to use and needn't interrupt the flow of lovemaking as people fear. Slipping on a condom isn't going to stop you both steaming up the windows.

In the 1990s women are, fortunately, becoming more assertive in the sexual arena. It's vital not to succumb to pressure from a man to act irresponsibly just because at some level you think, 'Oh, he'll leave me if I don't do what he wants.' If he did finish with you over such an issue, he would have failed a crucial test. Painful as this might be, it's better to know what he's like sooner rather than later. . . .

FURTHER DOWN THE LINE

Let's suppose you've survived all the early sexual hurdles and are now in an established relationship. So how's your sex life?

How often?

The first point to make is that there are no 'targets' for you to achieve here. People often worry about whether they're making love as often as other couples are, and perhaps they aren't, and oh dear, what does this mean?

Don't panic. Although, as I've said, sex surveys are tricky little beasts to carry out (is the sample representative? are people being truthful?) nevertheless it does seem clear that there are huge differences between couples.

To illustrate the point: a major American survey of happily married couples in the 1980s looked at their frequency of sex and how long a couple had been married. They found that in couples married up to two years, while 45 per cent were making love three or more times a week, 11 per cent were doing so only once a month to once a week. In couples married between two and ten years, 27 per cent were busy three times a week or more; 21 per cent once a month to once a week. In marriages of over ten years, while 18 per cent were still bending the bedsprings three times a week at least, 45 per cent were doing it one to three times a week, 22 per cent once a month to once a week, and 15 per cent once a month or less.

As you can see, there's a lot of variability. So that's cheering: don't fret if you're not doing it twice-nightly. There are no rules about frequencies of lovemaking that you need to worry about or compare yourself to.

But what if – regardless of the frequency of your lovemaking – you're not happy with that frequency? If you're both happy with, say, once a week – no problem. But if one of you is and one of you isn't, this might be a cause of friction.

If he wants more frequent sex than you do

The first question is: has this always been the case? And is it causing problems? If so, could some accommodation be reached?

Do you, in fact, know how often he *would* like to make love? You might think he wants it every five minutes because he keeps pestering you and dropping constant hints about the withering away of his member from lack of use. In fact he may be perfectly happy with a couple of times a week, and is only harping on so much because you get reluctant if it's more than once a fortnight.

So the first thing is to sit down and try to talk about it calmly. I know this can be difficult, but it could bring you both enormous benefits. Discussing what to do about sex can generally improve the quality of communication between the two of you. And it may be that upping your rate of intercourse will cheer up your partner and so benefit the relationship and yourself.

Find out what frequency he'd be happy with. You could say something like 'I feel you wish we made love more often than we do. I truly want to know what you'd like.' And no, you won't accept dismissive jokes of the 'five times a night, darling, heh-heh' variety.

Then think about how you'd feel about (say) twice a week. If you're not keen, do you think this might be rectifiable?

– Is the real reason you're not keen because he doesn't give you the stimulation you need to have fun and have orgasms? If so, you need – gently – to let him know (see 'Perking up your sex life' on page 150). If you're considering making love more often, he'll need to know what he can do to make it more pleasurable for you. I'm certainly not suggesting that you lie back and think of England in a bored and martyred fashion twice a week. But if you enjoy it more, then twice a week might seem just fine. . . .

– Do you think you might be a bit erotophobic? Do you respond to 'erotic cues' (nudity, masturbation, premarital intercourse, contraception and so on) with anxiety, guilt, fear, shame or embarrassment?

If so, why might you have learned to react this way? The American social psychologists Robert Baron and Donn Byrne put it this way: 'A young child may quickly discover that certain parts of the body should not be exposed or discussed, that a negative response to sexual scenes on TV amuses his or her parents, or that parents kiss or embrace only when they believe no one is looking. A child may also discover at some point that it feels good to touch the forbidden parts of the body.'

The greater your erotophobia, the less likely you are to discuss sex and the less frequently you'll have intercourse. If you do think your deep-rooted feelings about sex might be damaging your life and main relationship, you might want some assistance to reduce your anxieties and guilt. Ask your GP to refer you to a suitable chartered clinical psychologist or counsellor.

Now let's suppose that he wants more frequent sex than you do – but that this has happened recently, whereas previously you were quite evenly matched. It could be that his lust for you has increased (rather flattering); but if this is a long-standing relationship, a more likely explanation is that your lust for him is sagging rather.

– Is it that you are just exhausted with the day-to-day practicalities of life? If so, you need to address this. It won't be affecting your sexual appetite alone, but also your relationship generally and possibly your personal health.

If it's that you work too hard, maybe you need to think about things such as: your priorities in life, whether or not you're bad at delegating, whether or not you need to learn some time management skills.

If it's the fact that you work outside the home and like hell inside it too – particularly if there are children – then negotiating inequities, as I've already discussed, is vital.

If you're feeling stressed or depressed, this could be at the root of it.

– Are you feeling angry and resentful with your partner for some reason? Such feelings can be real killers of one's sexual urges. If that's the problem, tackle them and sort them out before they poison your whole relationship.

If you want more frequent sex than he does

Again, the first question is – has this always been the case? If so, then you can try the reverse of the advice above. Tell him gently that you'd really like to make love more often, and are there things you could do that would make it very pleasurable for him? If you think that he might possibly be erotophobic, to the extent of harming your relationship, then he too might benefit from seeking some professional advice.

But what if you want more frequent sex than he does – and this is a recent happening? Of course, it could be that you've had some thrilling upsurge in your sexual longings for your long-standing partner. If so, once he's got over the shock, as long as he enjoys it too he might be perfectly happy to make love more often.

What is more likely, unfortunately, is that it's his lusts which aren't burning quite as brightly as before. But there's no need for immediate panic. For instance, it could be that:

– He may be tired because of overwork. The same advice

about priorities, delegation and time management, apply
to him as to you.

- He may be feeling very stressed: work problems, money
difficulties, anything. So that you don't take his lessening of
sexual interest personally and start behaving in a way that
makes him feel even more stressed (being, say, snappy or
distant), try to find out what's troubling him. Then you can
help him work out ways of coping with the source of his stress.

- He could be depressed: feeling a failure at work, suffering
from a recent bereavement – there are many possibilities.

- He could be feeling sexually rather bored. To illustrate the
point: American psychologists have looked at people who
were either dating or newly married, and asked them
which of certain specific behaviours they would like more
or less of from their partner. The men more than the
women wanted their partners: (a) to engage in more experimental sex (b) to engage in more impulsive sex (c) to
initiate sex more (d) to play a dominant role more often.

  The women, on average, wanted a little more of these
things from their partner – but the men wanted significantly more than they did.

  This study was carried out on people at a relatively early
stage of their relationships – so it's reasonable to suppose
that, in couples of longer standing, these findings might
apply even more strongly.

- It could be just that he's getting a bit older (see page 155
for the question of the effects of aging).

- It could be that he's responding to how you have been
behaving towards him. I believe that when we're trying to
work out what's behind some shift in our partner's behaviour, we often severely underestimate the role that we
ourselves might have played in it.

The possibilities here are legion. Have you been neglecting
him of late because of work and/or children? Might you have
upset him by blurting out that your lovemaking together
could act as a perfect timer for a soft-boiled egg? Have you

been making too many enthusiastic remarks about the size of the pecs on that TV Gladiator, when your beloved has the body of a cornstalk?

All I can suggest is that it might be worth doing a mental review of whether or not *you* have been behaving to *him* differently in some way, and whether or not this could connect with his lessening of sexual interest in you.

This links into the most worrying possibility. It could be, I fear, that his lessening of sexual desire is something to do with how he's feeling about you: anger, resentment, increasing detachment and indifference. There is, too, the possibility that he has found someone else.

You may be sure in your own mind that this is what it is. But it's easy to deceive ourselves, if we are prone to insecurity and feelings of low self-worth. So be sure that none of the other possibilities applies before you reach the most worrying conclusion.

If you fear that's what it is, I am sure that by now you know what I'm going to say. Unpleasant things don't disappear because you don't talk about them. Even in the worst case scenario, you often hear of people saying, 'Well, I knew he was having an affair, and I felt dreadful, but I thought it was just a fling and if I kept quiet it would burn itself out and everything would be OK.'

The trouble is, what happens if you follow this line of thinking through to its logical conclusion? If it's a 'fling that will burn itself out', this entirely begs the question of why it happened in the first place. Those causes will probably still be present even if the affair does blow over. So what's going to make *them* right again? If untouched, might they not just burst out again in another fling for him? And more pain for you?

You may, of course, fear precipitating a crisis, and that he will walk out and leave you with, perhaps, two young children and no job. In such a case, what you can do is sit down and realistically think through your options.

When we feel anxious, angry, fearful or hurt, it's hard to think clearly. But it would help you if you could try.

One good way which psychologists have suggested to help people think clearly through complicated decisions is to take a piece of paper, and at the top write a horizontal row of column headings. You need one column for each of your options. Before you draw the columns, be sure that you have thought creatively about *all* your possible options. For instance: talk to him; look for a job; go home to mother. Then divide each column into two smaller columns, labelled 'for' and 'against'. List under 'for' all the arguments you can think of in favour of that option; and under 'against' all the arguments you can drum up against that option.

This is a great technique for encouraging you to think creatively about your situation, to explore all the arguments and to clarify your thinking. You may, indeed, see more than one course of action open to you which you can pursue simultaneously.

And if you do feel that you'd rather talk to him than carry on through months of anxiety and misery – well, at least it gives you an opportunity to get to the root of the matter and so have a chance of sorting it out.

Sexual dissatisfaction

One of the reasons why one of you might want to make love more than the other could as I've suggested above, be purely sexual. That is, one of you isn't enjoying it that much.

In some couples, both partners may not be enjoying it that much. 'Sex? Shopping? Er, wait while I fetch my purse.'

So what if your love life isn't particularly pleasurable? Why might this be? Perhaps one or both of you has a specific sexual difficulty; or it could be for more general psychological reasons, such as lack of communication. I shall look at each of these in turn.

Specific sexual problems

Details of the various types of 'sexual dysfunction', and their causes and treatment, are extremely complex and outside the scope of this book. Broadly speaking, sexual disorders fall into three categories: of desire, arousal and orgasm. (It's possible, of course, to have difficulties at more than one stage.)

For women:

- *Desire.* You may feel simply uninterested in sex. Women experience problems with sexual desire more often than men do.
- *Arousal.* You may have difficulty become sexually excited.
- *Orgasm.* Even if you are sexually aroused, you may be unable to reach – or have difficulty reaching – orgasm.

Rarer occurrences are problems such as vaginismus, where the muscles of the vagina go into involuntary spasm. This impedes, or even prevents, penetration.

For men:

- *Desire.* He may feel no – or little – desire for sex.
- *Arousal.* He may be impotent. Impotence is now referred to as 'erectile dysfunction' by medical professionals and psychologists, because it has fewer negative connotations. It means either being unable to get an erection, or failing to keep it long enough for intercourse to take place, or having difficulty in doing so.
- *Orgasm.* He may have no trouble getting aroused and having an erection. But he may have trouble with ejaculation. The most common problem is ejaculating prematurely. More rarely, he may suffer from retarded ejaculation. This means that, though he has an erection, he cannot ejaculate – or has difficulty ejaculating – during intercourse. This may happen even if he's able to ejaculate when he is stimulated by hand or mouth.

Some people may have what's called a 'primary' dysfunction – i.e. they've always had it. But for others, the dysfunction is 'secondary' – they used not to have it, but they do now.

There are many possible causes of sexual difficulties. Within an individual, several factors may be operating.

- *Physical.* The problem may be partly or wholly physical. Painful intercourse ('dyspareunia') in either men or women, for instance, quite often has some physical cause. Diabetes mellitus and certain drugs, amongst other things, can sometimes cause erectile dysfunction.
- *Physical plus psychological.* Sometimes both physical and psychological factors can be involved, for instance where a physically caused difficulty is made a great deal worse by the person's anxiety about it.
- *Psychological – from the past.* There could be psychological causes which have their roots in the person's past. For example: a repressive home background where sex was regarded as 'dirty'; being sexually abused as a child; or sexual trauma, such as rape, as an adult.
- *Psychological – from current factors outside the relationship.* As already mentioned, if either partner is stressed, depressed, exhausted or anxious for reasons which are nothing at all to do with the relationship (work, money, bereavement, etc.), this can affect sexual functioning.
- *Psychological – from the occasional 'failure'.* It's possible to create a self-fulfilling prophecy for yourself. Most women, for instance, don't have an orgasm every time they make love. Most men will occasionally fail to get an erection. What can turn these quite natural occurrences into a full-blown problem is anxiety about future performance. This anxiety then *does* inhibit your future sexual responses. And what you feared has come true. 'Oh no, I didn't have an orgasm.' Next time: 'Oh help, I didn't have an orgasm last time, he'll *die* if I don't have one this time. I feel so tense. Uh-oh, no orgasm again.'

A British study of men illustrates the point too. Two-thirds of those who reported having problems with erections said the difficulty had righted itself without help. The most common reason the men gave (cited by just over half of them) was that they'd *stopped worrying* about not getting an erection.

- *Psychological – 'fear of failure'*. Both men and women can suffer fear of failure in the sexual arena, known as 'performance anxiety'. Men in particular may have over-high expectations of themselves, and this can bring trouble. Their anxieties may make them particularly prone to a self-fulfilling prophecy.
- *Psychological – in the relationship itself*. As I discussed above, the root cause of the difficulty may lie in the person's feelings about their partner and the relationship.
- *Technical*. The cause here might be to do with the partner – but not in the emotional sense. It may be that the person 'with the problem' isn't receiving enough sexual stimulation.

Many women, for example, say they do not get enough foreplay. Men are not always as knowledgeable as you'd think they might be. They may think that physical penetration should automatically be enough to get any woman excited any time. (Wrong. . . .) Not all men know that women often take more arousing than men do. They do not always know about how important the clitoris is for female arousal; the clitoris has a greater number of sensitive nerve endings than the vagina. In fact, increasing numbers of jokes are being made these days about the need to provide many men with a route map.

What to do?

Obviously, this section is not intended to be a self-diagnosis manual – sexual difficulties are too complex to be dealt with in such a manner. What it is designed to do is to alert you to the various possibilities. If you're feeling unmoved, or his erection has the staying power of a politician's promise, it can help to be aware of the wide variety of possible causes. This might prevent either or both of you getting into an unnecessary state and letting the situation start grating away at your relationship.

Very simply, if the problem is of long standing, I would advise seeking professional help. Your or your partner's doctor may be the best first port of call. He or she can then take the necessary steps to work out if the problem is primarily physical or basically psychological, very probably stemming from the person's distant past. If the latter, the person with the 'primary dysfunction' can then be referred for appropriate counselling or therapy.

If the problem is of more recent date, you need to review the possibilities. You may have strong suspicions about the true cause. Your partner may have just lost his job. You know your man thinks 'foreplay' is something to do with golf. You're well aware that you've been growing apart lately.

If you are pretty certain as to the cause, you can tackle it.

- If you or your partner are labouring under outside pressures, those need to be addressed as far as they can be. In the meantime, until those pressures lift, the other partner needs to refrain from placing the sufferer under additional burdens – feeling sexually inadequate and fearful that they're about to be abandoned for being so utterly useless in is bed.
- What if you reckon that the basic cause is utterly unnecessary anxiety – about the odd failure, or about sexual performance generally? If that applies to you, the mere knowledge of what you're doing might be enough to help you start relaxing over the whole business. No one has perfect sex lives, and the odd glitch is absolute normal. Nor is an in-depth knowledge of the Kama Sutra essential for a rollicking and passionate sex life.

If you think it's your partner who's the anxious one, you can try to reassure him in the same way as you would if it were yourself who was fretting. Just talking about the issue may help. In a British study of men having problems with erections, the top cause – mentioned by nearly half of them – was that they felt they couldn't talk to their partner about sexual matters.

– If you believe that the root cause lies in the fact that your relationship hasn't been going too well lately, then that will have to be addressed. Talk to him, using the communication skills described earlier. And it may be time for some repair work (see Chapter 7).

– If the cause is, frankly, technical, then I'd advise injecting some sexual knowledge for you both into the situation. Bookshops positively bulge with books on sex (more than on relationships, it seems to me . . .). Why not choose any of those, with pictures, diagrams and route maps to the clitoris if necessary. If your partner has a common problem, say premature ejaculation (which is probably distressing him as well as frustrating you dreadfully), these books usually have explicit suggestions for tackling such things, with detailed instructions and pictures. The 'squeeze' technique, for instance, is a popular idea for combatting the old p.e. Obviously, don't thrust the chosen tome into your partner's hands saying, 'Darling, I think you'd better read this'.

Try to be a bit tactful here.

You could say something like, 'I was browsing in the bookshop today, and I thought "Gosh, there's all these shelves and shelves of sex books, and I thought it might be fun to buy one and see what it said! I wonder what sort of things they suggest. . . ."'

But – and this is very important – if in any doubt, or if the problem persists, it would be wise to consult your doctor. If the cause *is* physical, that needs to be checked out. If the cause is entirely psychological, you can be reassured of the fact that there *is* no physical problem, and receive appropriate help if necessary. You could, for example, be referred for relationships counselling and/or sex therapy as a couple. (Counselling or therapy of any sort won't always work, but going to a qualified practitioner *can* help. So it might be worth at least giving it a go if it seems appropriate.) Or if one partner is under particular stress, he or she may be referred for some individual professional help.

Don't let difficulties which are hurting one or both of you, and potentially your relationship, go on and on without being confronted.

Sexual difficulties and relationship happiness

Of course, it's important to say that sexual difficulties won't always damage your relationship at all. One study of British men, for instance, found that those with problems with erections or ejaculation were more likely to be sexually dissatisfied, but they were *not* more likely to be unhappy in their marriages. This wasn't a representative sample (they were a particularly satisfied bunch), but it makes the point that sexual dissatisfaction doesn't always have to mean marital dissatisfaction.

Indeed, some people have sexual difficulties and yet say they are satisfied with their sex lives. A study of couples not currently seeking therapy (but again, not a representative sample) found that nearly two-thirds of the women reported some degree of dysfunction – mainly trouble in getting excited and in reaching orgasm. But only a fifth of them said they were sexually dissatisfied. Perhaps they were still getting important rewards from their lovemaking: physical expressions of love and affection, which made them feel loved and wanted; cuddling, stroking, and tenderness afterwards.

It's been suggested, too, that sexual trouble may be less likely to make marital trouble if the couple feel able to discuss it and try to solve the problem constructively together. Indeed, the main reason some psychologists think sex therapy works – when it does – is because it has encouraged the couple to *talk* to each other.

On the other hand, a couple's sex life can actually be fine, and yet the relationship itself is not. Sex therapists have pointed out that some couples can carry on having satisfactory sex right up to their separation. So sexual satisfaction in itself won't necessarily save an otherwise wobbly relationship.

So even if sexual dissatisfaction won't always damage your relationship, nor sexual satisfaction rescue it, this doesn't mean you shouldn't try to have as good a time sexually as you can. After all, even if sexual dodginess won't always harm things, it might do; and even if sexual happiness won't necessary be enough to save a relationship that is sliding down the plughole, it sure as hell isn't going to do any harm. Research studies find that close, intimate marriages tend to have satisfactory sex; and less happy marriages to have less pleasurable sex. This doesn't in itself reveal what's causing what, but it's reasonable to assume that sexual and marital happiness – and unhappiness – may often feed into each other. And anyway, why shouldn't you both have as much fun in bed as you can? For its own sake, as well as to boost and reinforce the bond between you.

So, let's say your sex life is ticking along, with no major difficulties as such; but you sense it could be a bit more fireworky. What can you do?

Perking up your sex life

Having a good sex life isn't a matter of following sexual instructions like a cookbook. Take the Kama Sutra, turn to position 689, the Congress of the Cockroach, take hold of his left leg, twist it round your right ankle, no, no, left a bit. . . . Enough to turn you into a celibate for life, once the bandages come off.

At the other extreme, unless you watch it, there is a danger that things can become pretty routine. What you do, when, how; and you could set a stopwatch by the number of seconds it takes him to fall asleep afterwards. Not good.

You need to know the answers to four questions:

1 Am I doing the things to him that he would like me to do?

2 Is he doing the things to me that I would like him to do?

3 Are there things that he might like if only we tried it?

4 Are there things that I might like if only we tried it?

To find the answers:

1 Ask him.

a You can ask straightforwardly – 'Are there things you'd like me to do that I don't?' – and see what he says. Remember to 'actively listen' (see page 62) – don't get so worked up worrying about what he might say, and whether he might criticize you, that you don't actually take in what he's talking about.

Some of the things he suggests you may be happy to do (and wonder why you hadn't thought of it before); some you may be prepared to try. If, however, he suggests things that you really don't like the sound of, then it's better to be straight with him. A sex life that's great for one partner while making the other person feel a bit queasy is not a recipe for a happy life, frankly. At the absolute extreme, if you found that your partner's strongest sexual leanings were towards practices that you find distasteful, you would need to do some hard thinking about the long-term viability of the relationship.

However, let's hope that you would discover things that are fine by you. Indeed, as well as making him happy – which is cheering for you too – you might find you enjoy them a lot into the bargain.

b If there are things you occasionally do and are not sure how he feels about them, then you can say – as you're in the process of licking his knee or whatever it is – 'How does this feel?' If you ask too directly, 'Do you like this?' he may, bless him, say 'yes' to be polite. But if in fact all it does is tickle, he'll be more able to tell you if you ask as an open-ended question.

2 So – what about you? Is he doing the things to you that *you* want?

Very possibly he isn't – or not for long enough. A cursory ten-second focus on your clitoris, say, may be much too brief. Or you might like him to kiss your back all over. Or . . .

It can be tricky to come clean because people fear embarrassment, making a fool of themselves, inadvertently hurting or offending the other person. But part of a deep, intimate bond is the ability to make yourselves vulnerable to each other. By revealing your true needs you can deepen that bond. This can, too, encourage him to talk to you freely in a similar fashion. However, because this *is* a delicate area, and people's self-esteem can be easily squashed between the sheets, you do have to tread a bit carefully.

An American psychologist, Janet Shibley Hyde, has looked at communication techniques specifically in the context of sexual relationships. These techniques can be applied to any topic, and I have already talked about the principles of good communication. But given how extremely difficult sex talk can be, it might be helpful to emphasize and illustrate some tactics here.

a *Levelling and editing.* The first step, and often the hardest, is, as Hyde puts it, to 'tell your partner what you are feeling by stating your thoughts clearly, simply, and honestly'. What do you want and need? What do – and don't – you like? But you do have to edit out anything that would deliberately hurt him. He will be sensitive in this department, and doesn't want to learn that he has the sexual expertise of a wombat.

b *Good messages.* He'll be less likely to go on the defensive if you use the word 'I' rather than 'you'. 'I feel a bit unhappy because I don't often have orgasms' is better than 'You never give me orgasms.'

c *Documenting.* Where you can, give a specific example. This will help your partner to understand what the problem is, especially if you can also give him a concrete suggestion

about what he could do about it. For instance: 'It was
lovely last night, but I didn't quite come at the end. I was
so close, and I think what would have done it would have
been if you'd rubbed my clitoris for just a couple of
minutes more.'

d *Positive communication.* Don't forget to tell him occasionally that that really *was* wonderful, your legs have entirely
forgotten how to walk and you feel terrific. You don't
want to open your mouth during lovemaking only to
groan (with passion) or moan (talk about difficulties). . . .

3 Are there things that he might like if only you tried it?

a Ask him. Perhaps he has fantasies that it might be interesting to hear about? Perhaps he's had ideas about things
he'd like to try but has never mentioned them? Again,
whether or not you go along with these things is up to
you. But if he suggests something you're not sure you like
the idea of, but you can understand why it occurred to
him, then say so. *Validating* is part of good communication. Hyde says: 'This means that you communicate to
your partner that, given his or her point of view, you can
see why he or she thinks a certain way. It doesn't mean
that you agree with your partner or that you're giving in.'
But to indicate that you understand, even if you don't feel
the same way, at least shows that you respect his right to
hold a different view and won't make him feel such a prize
idiot. And it makes it possible at least to discuss his idea a
bit. You never know, his thoughts about painting you with
chocolate mousse and licking it off might be worth a
moment of your consideration (as long as he washed the
sheets). (If his ideas are in fact extremely dear to him and
extremely off-putting to you, then, as I said above, you
might have to put in some serious thinking about whether
this relationship can hold up if you have such different
approaches to sexuality.)

b Use your imagination. Look at the various bits of his

body and try to think what you could do to them that he might like. Give it a little go and see what happens. Usually appropriate moaning or other signs of appreciation will tell you if you're on the right track; otherwise you can enquire.

c If you haven't already bought a good book on sex (see above), then why not do so? After all, they're jammed with information, ideas, techniques, guides as to which bits of a man's body are the most sensitive, and so on. After all, detailed sexual knowledge isn't something you were born with, and school sex education and a few biology lessons about rabbits aren't going to provide all the necessary info. So buying such a book can be rather a sensible idea. In fact, Janet Hyde suggests that you can use such a book to 'break the ice'. If you both read the book and discuss it together, it might help you and him to raise specific topics – such as oral sex – that have previously been too shy-making.

4 Are there things that *you* might like if only you tried it? If so, apply the above advice to yourself. Tell him; use your imagination; buy a sex manual to give you some more ideas. And remember, in terms of your health and figure, chocolate mousse is better out than in.

But don't go to the other extreme, and start building up huge expectations of yourself and of him. Sex is not going to be brilliant every time, and you're certainly not going to be able to dream up a different sexual technique on a daily basis. No matter how long you've been together, sex can be an expression of – and fuel for – your love for each other; and it's meant to be fun. Don't set it up as another major life challenge. Get promotion, earn £50,000 a year, become the best sex partner in the world. Unrealistic expectations and pressures would finish you off altogether. All I'm saying is that, with a bit of extra knowledge and imaginative effort, you could both have a bit more fun.

Getting older

You may fear that, with the passage of years, there's in the end nothing you can do to prevent the total seizing-up of your sex life. But there is no need to fret.

It's true that research studies show that frequency of intercourse tends to drop over the years. Certain aspects of the aging process can have an effect. Sexual interest is likely to decline somewhat. For men, too, erections tend to develop more slowly, and they hold for less time. For women, the menopause can bring some changes, but these could be less noticeable than you fear.

There's some evidence that any damaging effects of the menopause on your love life may often be more psychological than physiological. For instance, if you mistakenly believe that the menopause means the end of your sex life, or that you're 'no longer a woman', then you might bring about a self-fulfilling prophecy. You think all the fun's over; and so it is. But there's no need to psych yourself into a few decades of quite unnecessary celibacy.

Any physiological changes of the menopause needn't be that bad, either. For instance:

- There's been a lot of talk about 'vaginal dryness'; in fact, this troubles less than 10 per cent of women. A greater number do report some loss of vaginal lubrication – but lubricants are available to compensate.
- There can be some shrinkage of the vagina. But there's evidence that this is lessened if you're still having inter-course regularly.

There is, indeed, no need to despair. So your lovemaking may drop somewhat in frequency, and become perhaps a gentler and less frantic business. But, as the British psychiatrist John Bancroft has pointed out, there is no need for it to be any less enjoyable. The fact that you no longer feel the desperate urgency to do it on the hall carpet doesn't mean it might not still be pretty good on your orthopaedic bed.

In fact, the evidence is that, if you've had a good sex life, the chances are that you'll be able to carry on having an enjoyable time well past retirement. Indeed, according to Janet Hyde, quite a few couples still have active sex lives into their eighties.

So there's no need to fear that, however good your sex life is now, it's all going to drain away like air out of a punctured tyre. And if you feel it's not quite good enough now, well, as you've seen, there are steps you can take about that. . . .

7

Repairing

It is perfectly possible for a relationship that could work – or has been working – to be eaten away by a myriad of factors, as we have seen. If you fear that the health of your relationship is now down to danger level, what can you do to try to make it right again?

When relationships are going wrong, many people do not respond in ways that might have a chance to put things back on course. The American psychologist Caryl Rusbult and her colleagues have looked at reactions when relationships hit a sticky patch, and classified them into four types:

1 *Exit*: For instance: separating, threatening to leave, or yelling at your partner.
2 *Neglect*: Ignoring the partner or spending less time together, avoiding discussing problems, treating the partner poorly (being cross with him or her), criticizing the partner for things unrelated to the real problem, or just letting things fall apart.
3 *Loyalty*: Closing your eyes, metaphorically speaking, and waiting and hoping that 'it's just a phase' and 'things will right themselves'.
4 *Voice*: Discussing problems, seeking help from a friend or therapist, suggesting solutions, changing oneself, or urging one's partner to change.

Clearly responses 1 and 2 are not going to help matters; and it's not yet clear from research when 'loyalty' might be a good idea. But in my view, it's a risky option. Root causes are not being addressed, the situation might deteriorate, and hanging around for months waiting for him to start talking to you again is going to do nothing for your happiness and self-esteem – and may indeed start to make you feel angry and resentful.

But as you can see, the 'voice' option is by no means bound to occur. Wherever the problem lies (or, more likely, problems), it may have to be you who takes the initiative to sort it out. The evidence is that men tend to react neglectfully to relationship problems more often than women do. (The evidence as to whether or not they start savaging or terminating the relationship – the 'exit' option – more than women do is, however, equivocal.)

The first question to ask yourself is – do you want to sort it out? This is a judgement which only you can make. But think about it hard. If it's been a mistake from the beginning and has got worse, you might think it's better to stop now. (It's noticeable that most divorces take place after only a few years of marriage.) If he's beating you up and won't get help for it – well, you know what I think about that. But if you've had a good and loving relationship which has slipped off the rails somehow, you might well think that the present situation is worth some repair attempts.

So, in a first basic survey of the situation, where do you think the problem lies?

1 Is it that his behaviour has not changed, but, over the years, you've got fed up with it? It may be devotion to his work, his golf, his unsociability or any number of things.
2 Has his behaviour changed in a way that you don't like? Either generally – e.g. he works much harder and drinks much more – or in relation to you? Has he withdrawn psychologically (and probably sexually), or has he become argumentative and aggressive?

3 Has your behaviour changed – either generally or specifically in relation to him?
4 Has your behaviour not changed, but he has started to
make negative remarks about it? 'Why do you spend such
long hours at that office?' 'Why won't you ever come and
watch me play cricket?'

HIS BEHAVIOUR HASN'T CHANGED, BUT YOU'VE BECOME FED UP

Aspects of the other person's behaviour that don't trouble us
much at first can, over time, become wearing. So – is this
behaviour alterable?

It may well be that it's more alterable than you think it is.
Often people act in a certain way out of habit, and may not
even realize how increasingly tired of it you are getting. They
play squash three nights a week because they always have.
They may not get home until 9pm every night because
they're ambitious, in a high-pressure job and afraid of losing
it – and they can't remember when these things were not the
case. They may say they don't want to go out in the evening
because they're too tired.

Whatever the difficulties are you will need to tell him how
they are making you feel. Then you can see whether or not
he is prepared to try to change those aspects of his behaviour
which are upsetting you. Otherwise, you may simply crack
one day, leave him a 'your dinner is in the gerbil' note and
storm off to mother.

In this scenario, he will be utterly bemused and wonder
what he did wrong. So tell him what the matter is rather
than making him feel as though he's stepped on a psychological mine. If he refuses to listen to you or to do what he can
to mend matters, then for you it could be decision-making
time.

HIS BEHAVIOUR HAS CHANGED IN A WAY YOU DON'T LIKE

Generally

Perhaps, rather than you becoming exasperated by some of his long-standing behaviour patterns, what's happened is that he *has* changed. This could be for the better as far as you are concerned: he might have become more laid-back, tolerant, kinder to the gerbil. But the risk is that perhaps it's been for the worse, from your – and possibly from his – point of view.

Suppose he's become work-obsessed. Or sport-obsessed. Or alcohol-obsessed. Or. . . .

If problems have developed such as alcoholism, addictive gambling or anything life-ruining of that nature, you do need to persuade him to seek professional help. Otherwise it's not going to be just his life that's ruined, but yours too.

But perhaps the problem is something that you reckon is not life-ruining in that sense, but is mega-upsetting to you. Again, you must tell him. Don't *hint*. Don't say, 'I'm getting rather tired of trying to get the stains out of your rugby shirt.' Say, 'I'm feeling lonely and neglected when you're out so much at the weekends.' Keep reminding yourself that the man is not a telepath. Use all those communication and conflict management skills. Don't keep miserably quiet for five years before cracking. Life's too short.

Once you've had your say, he needs to be encouraged to tell you *why* he's been doing what he has been doing. Has he been working so late because he's scared of losing his job? If so, talk it through. Is that a realistic fear? Is working so late going to save him anyway if redundancy is on the cards? OK, if he's made redundant, what's the worst that could happen? So would it kill you to live in a smaller house?

Obviously this is just an example – I only want to make the point that, whatever his reasons are, they need to be thought through to the limit. Often people do things for reasons which are, when looked at closely, either unnecessary or dealable with in some other way. If, for instance, the real reason he plays rugby all weekend is that he doesn't know how else to relax from his desperately stressful job, then perhaps you could make a few alternative suggestions. . . . And is there some means of making his working life *less* stressful anyway? Regarding this as a problem that you can discuss and try to solve together could help to draw you closer again.

In relation to you

The two most likely patterns, broadly speaking, are either that he has pulled back from you, or that you are constantly in conflict – anything from mild sniping to full-blown chronic rowing.

If he has withdrawn from you, what are you to do? If you tackle him head on at this point about what's wrong, there's a risk that he may already be so disaffected that he won't tell you. Indeed, it is always possible that he doesn't have a very clear understanding himself.

Men's discussions of the kicking of oval balls and economic crises can be so sophisticated. But ask them to talk about their relationship with their loved one – a rather more vital figure in their lives, you'd think, than England's scrum half or the prime minister – and things don't look so hot.

An American study illustrates the point. The researcher, Robert Martin, asked male and female students (aged twenty-eight on average) to describe, in their own words, a romantic relationship that they had been or were involved in. It transpired that women used a greater variety of concepts when talking about relationships than the men did.

Women commented more on similarities and differences between themselves and their partner; on typical things done with the partner, such as going to the movies, talking about goals in life; on qualities, assumptions and rules of the relationship ('We expect each other to tell the truth', 'Our relationship will last forever'); and on the personal history of either partner, or the history of the relationship, with reference to how this affects the relationship now ('We both had lousy relationships with our parents and that has helped us to understand each other').

But, I hear you ask, does this matter? Unfortunately, another study of 'relationship awareness' implies that it does. This researcher, Linda Acitelli, interviewed forty-two couples who had been married between two and five years, and asked them open-ended questions about 'the nice [and] the unpleasant things in your lives since you've been married'. The wives talked more about their relationship than their husbands did; but the more the husbands did talk about the relationship, the greater was the wives' satisfaction with their marriages.

So it's probably best to assume that the initiative for repairing the cracks in your relationship lies in your court. But if you're not satisfied, and he's not talking, you might have to lay a bit of groundwork before starting the talking process. Listen for clues; provide a few rewards; and see if you can cut down on his costs.

Listen for clues

When someone's feeling fed up with their relationship, it's quite common, according to social psychologist Steve Duck, for this to leak through hints and little needling remarks. 'Only 9pm and you're *home!*' 'I think I'm going to put my private parts in a car boot sale. Maybe someone else'll get some use out of them.'

Though these remarks may be disguised as jokes, the lack of genuine humorous crinkles round his eyes could give the game away. So start to tune in to these dropped hints. It may be that, once you know what's bothering him, you can take steps to alter what you are doing. Even by making some small changes to accommodate him, this might make him feel that at least you are trying. As you're slaving over your word processor in the only pool of light in a darkened office, tell yourself this is no way for a grown woman to live. If, in contrast, the office is still brightly lit and buzzing at 8pm, announce you've got a home to go to. Think to yourself that your colleagues are the ones who should get a life. You've got one, thanks. And you'd like to keep it.

If you make an obvious effort to solve what seems to be troubling your partner, he might be more receptive when you grasp the bull by the horns and ask him to discuss it directly. He then might feel more inclined to tell you his true feelings about what's been happening. What's more, he may also – with your gentle encouragement – feel able to tell you if there are other things troubling him too. The truth is that if he is currently not very happy with your relationship, there is likely to be more than one reason. So while he's about it, it would be good in the long run – if painful now – to hear the lot.

I think that sometimes all the aspects troubling a person coagulate into one shapeless mass, and he or she can't separate them out. All they know is that they feel angry and fed up. Perhaps they can pinpoint one or two specific things – but really there are several more lurking dangerously in the mix. But if you have been carefully on the lookout for clues, you might be able to help your partner identify these. Given that men seem to think about relationships in a less complex way than women, you might find yourself better placed to try to stand back and assess what else might be bothering him. For example:

- You can compare the way you live your lives now compared to how you were in the first flushes of love and happiness. What are the differences? In amount of time spent together? In the extent of your social life? In how much you talked? In anything else?
- You can think back to when you first noticed a withdrawal on his part. Did it coincide with any other event, do you think?

Setting up a few hypotheses of your own might also help to sensitize you to clues that you hadn't properly picked up on before.

Play psychological detective as much as you can. But, most important, encourage him to talk for as long and as often as he needs. That way, it should – let's hope – all come spilling out over time. Once he realizes he can talk about his real thoughts and feelings without you throwing a major wobbly (remember conflict management), he should be gradually encouraged to reveal them. This may not happen in one session, and is much more likely to take a number of conversations.

Provide rewards

Think back to the importance of rewards. Start asking yourself some hard questions. How rewarding do you think your relationship is for him at the moment? This might be really painful for you, and it's a question that I think people often don't ask enough. It's one that, ideally, everyone in a relationship should ask regularly, because knowing and acting on the answers can help to keep the relationship fuelled. Certainly at this point, where you have become seriously disturbed, it is wise to force yourself to ask those difficult questions. For instance:

1 Is your life too routine and predictable? When, say, did you last go out for a meal and chat and make each other laugh – and no, *not* to your local Italian as usual?
2 When did you last:

- compliment him?
- give him an unexpected hug?
- say 'I love you'?
- initiate sex?

3 When did you last have some serious fun together? Can you remember things that he used particularly to enjoy and that he hasn't done or had for a long time? Then you

could try to give a few of them to him. . . . Whether it's a trip to the reptiles at the zoo or a long session of back massage, it might start to remind him of how good things have been in the past – and could be again.

A word of warning here: be careful to *target* what you do carefully; don't just randomly suggest things. Don't say, 'We never have dinner parties any more; let's have Sylvia and Norman round.' If Sylvia can't stop talking about her hysterectomy and Norman about his new Black & Decker workbench, and both topics give your partner a pain, this will just make things worse. If you're not speaking much, it might be better to go and do something which you both used to relish and which offers something to talk about. Going to a modern art gallery and having a laugh over whether or not the mud-encrusted wheelbarrow in the corner is an exhibit or not; whatever used to suit you as a couple in the past. It might seem strange to suggest that you need something to break the ice with your own partner – but it might be *just* what you need.

Reduce costs

Ask yourself what costs he might be suffering at the moment in your relationship. This again might be a difficult question to ask yourself, I know. But if you have been contributing to the problem – possibly without realizing fully what you were doing – it's better to face it. Otherwise how can you act to make things better? For example:

1 Do you think you might have been criticizing him in an undermining way? If so, try to catch yourself before these little darts shoot out. The trouble is, once people feel settled in a relationship, they get more relaxed about being critical. One research study found that, even in happy couples, partners are more prone to complaining to and criticizing each other than they are strangers, to whom they are considerate and express approval and agreement.

Even though we are supposed to be on our 'best behaviour' with strangers, and obviously you don't want to feel you have to watch every word with your partner, we don't want to assume the reverse – that our loved one will take whatever we choose to dish out. Marital happiness *is* linked with expressing positive, rather than negative, feelings and information.

2 Have you unconsciously withdrawn from him because he's been upsetting *you*, and you've been afraid to rock the boat by confronting this? If you have withdrawn from him, his own withdrawal may be mainly a reaction to *your* behaviour.

If he has not withdrawn from you because he is unhappy, the other main likelihood is that you are constantly rowing.

If he says something critical, have you been reacting badly – snapping at him or charging off? It's better to listen – it might be a partial clue to what's wrong. By remaining calm and asking him to tell you more about what he's feeling, you have a chance of tackling the problem. Otherwise you can both get into or perpetuate a negative cycle of criticism – snap/complain – more criticism. . . . Remember those? I know it's hard, but if you can bite your tongue and stick your ears out on stalks you've got a chance of pulling out of this nose dive.

YOUR BEHAVIOUR HAS CHANGED

Generally

Perhaps the core of the problem is that, over the years, you have changed in yourself.

How we are at sixteen is not necessarily how we're going to be at sixty-six. Evidence indicates that people can change and develop throughout life. If, as part of your change, you and your partner have been spending less and less time together and less and less time talking, you may have started to lose touch with each other and with how you're both seeing the world. As you start to move apart, you provide fewer and fewer rewards for each other, and maybe start to gain them elsewhere – perhaps in the triumphs of a new career or new social circle.

You may also have started to forget why you loved him in the first place, and how good the relationship once was. Human beings are great ones for reconstructing history, and it may be that in your current alienation you think to yourself, 'Well, it never was that good.' But it might have been.

Try to analyse what it is in your life and attitudes that has separated you from your partner – and whether he can share more with you than has been the case in the recent past. Have you got new friends whom he hasn't met? Are you telling him enough about what you're doing in the day? Does he understand how you *feel* about the new things in your life?

Perhaps, too, there are new elements which you could investigate together. As Robin Gilmour, a social psychologist, has suggested:

Couples . . . need to inject variety into their joint experience. Holidays, new ways of sharing sex, exploring new sports, hobbies and studies together are all useful strategies. Change that involves them both can help a couple to avoid, on the one hand, the strain of growing apart through a growing dissimilarity, and, on the other, the boredom of knowing so much about each other that there are no stimulating surprises.

And what about the things you used to do together that you once got a kick out of? Theatre visits? Midnight picnics? Being rubbed all over with baby oil? Going to football matches and yelling 'Here we go'? You could try to reinstitute the rewards *you* used to get out of the relationship, that you have both somehow let drop in the sweep of life and of change. You need to remind yourself – and him – of the good times. A partner who has become psychologically associated with nothing but routine and drudgery, as I've said, may no longer be valued as once he was.

At worst, it may be that you have each changed so much, in directions 180 degrees apart, that with the best will in the world neither of you can pull yourselves back together again.

But if the relationship was once good, then it's worth at least a try, isn't it?

In relation to him

Perhaps your feelings have gone beyond the point where you're even feeling very motivated to try to improve things. Perhaps you are still in the relationship now out of inertia, fear, not wanting to disturb the children. You may feel that you don't want to take any of the steps I have suggested above: talking to him about things that trouble you, taking action to increase the number of rewards you're getting out of the relationship and so on. But yet you're reading this book, so your motivation can't be quite dead yet.

What you may need to do, before taking any action, is to take a good look at your thought processes.

False attributions?

What are you *thinking* about your partner? Can he not seem to do anything right?

The core issue here is that when a partner acts (or doesn't act), there are several ways you might view the situation. An action by person A doesn't trigger an automatic reflex in person B. A does something negative, B is angry; A does something positive, B is pleased. How you react to actions by your partner depend on *what you think* about what he's done.

Say, for instance, that he arrives home terribly late without having phoned you. His dinner looks like a lump of charcoal. He will offer a explanation. 'I was stuck in a meeting with our most important client who's about to withdraw her business and I didn't dare leave the room to phone you/Miss Wiggins suddenly collapsed in hysterics over the death of her pet snake and I was the only person left in the office and I thought she might do herself a damage with a paperknife/ The traffic was backed up solidly behind a lorry that had just shed its load of horse manure.'

There are two major ways you might regard such explanations.

Approach 1

- You selfish unreliable bastard, this is typical, you always put work first, you don't love me.
- Who's more important, me or your secretary? I always seem to come last in your order of priorities. Anyway, knowing your office, it'd be a miracle if her paperknife were sharp enough even to slit an envelope.
- It's your story that's horse manure.

Approach 2

- Yeah, I understand. You've told me about that woman before. An unpredictable bitch with the patience of a Rottweiler. She could easily have stuck the boot in while you were out of the room for five seconds and you wouldn't be there to retrieve things.
- Oh, *poor* Miss Wiggins! She loved that snake with a passion. Obviously you wouldn't want to leave her alone for a second until she'd calmed down. Maybe you could buy a baby adder – that might cheer her up.
- That road is a nightmare – far too narrow to get past a mountain of horse droppings. Tell you what – let's buy you a mobile phone.

You see the difference? Approach 1 attributes the man's behaviour to some internal aspect of him as a person – his selfishness, unreliability, priorities or whatever. Approach 2 puts his action down to external circumstances that aren't destined perpetually to recur.

Psychological studies have found clear differences between distressed and happy couples in the way they regard each other's behaviour.

- *In unhappy couples*: you are more likely to attribute his negative actions to factors that are internal (due to the person himself), stable (unlikely to change) and global (likely to affect many other situations in the marriage too – he's late home today, so he'll forget our anniversary next week). You're also particularly likely to feel that your partner is fully responsible for what's happened: he is to blame, he did it out of malign intent and it reflects his selfish concerns.

  But what if he does something positive? Suppose he has, as a surprise, booked dinner at a new Chinese restaurant in town. In distressed marriages, the evidence is that you are more likely to reckon this is due to something external (determined by the situation or outside factors), unstable (temporary) and specific to this event (and unlikely to influence many other areas of the relationship). 'He must want to celebrate some triumph at work/He must be getting it on expenses/They must have a special offer on hen's feet.'

  As you can see, once you've fallen into this way of thinking, your partner will simply not be able to win whatever he does.

So how does it work in happy couples?

- *In happy couples*: the reverse pattern of attributions is more likely to occur. His not-too-great actions will be put down to something external, unstable and less global – 'The poor darling must have had a vile day at work.' His positive actions will more often be put down to internal, stable causes, which benefit many aspects of the marriage. 'He booked the restaurant because he is thoughtful/kind/considerate/fun-loving/spontaneous/-loves me.'

(It's worth pointing out here, by the way, that evidence indicates such attributions are most likely to occur for positive actions which are *unexpected*. Routine nice behaviour may come to be taken for granted. This is not a good idea – periodic open expressions of appreciation are. 'You're so *good* to me. I do appreciate it, you know.')

Of course, these attributions won't always occur, even in happy couples. One study has found that, compared to unhappy couples, happy ones have a more complex pattern of attributions. So while their overall style of thought about what the other does is significantly more benign, that doesn't mean that they won't sometimes think bad action = personal fault, and good action – well, can't rely on *that* happening again. . . . In contrast, couples in distressed marriages tend to have a more rigid way of making attributions. They're more prone to the pattern of thinking that says negative behaviour = bastard, and positive behaviour = aberration.

Of course, it is perfectly possible that the negative attributions you are making are perfectly true. Your man really *is* an unreliable selfish sod.

But what I am concerned about here is the case where this is not true (or at least is grossly exaggerated); where it is a product of a distorted pattern of thinking on your part which has built up over time. If it *is* distorted, it will almost certainly start to affect your actions. This, in turn, may have a bad effect on your partner's feelings and behaviour. If he's late and couldn't phone you because of something horrible and unavoidable, and you are (as he sees it, unjustifiably) furious with him, he's not going to be very happy either.

But what is causing what here? If you are feeling unhappy, you may well start making negative attributions if your man even breathes audibly. There is indeed evidence that a counter-productive pattern of attributions can result from marital dissatisfaction. But, although research is still at an early stage, what evidence there is implies that a tendency to think negatively about a partner's actions can *cause* dissatisfaction too. And perhaps the two feed into each other – the dissatisfaction and the negative attributions make each other worse and worse.

Your negative pattern of thinking could have been there from early on; unrealistic expectations of your partner and of relationships in general, researchers suggest, might have contributed to setting up such a pattern. So if you suspect you might have fallen into this particular psychological quicksand, what can you do?

Try to start checking what you are thinking when your partner does things – either negative or positive. If you catch yourself thinking bad thoughts whatever he's done, stop a moment. Think of *several* possible reasons why he might have acted this way, and try to assess the evidence for and against each reason. You might find that a calmer, more rational look at his behaviour will start to shift your automatic negative thinking.

For instance: he brings you an un-birthday present of an expensive new book which you had mentioned looked interesting.

You think: 'I bet he didn't buy this for me. Bet someone in the office bought it and regretted it and wanted to get rid of it.'

Or: 'He must be feeling guilty about something. Bet he's having an affair with that new receptionist who wears microskirts and flicks her hair about a lot.'

Try to think of some alternative explanations.

'That was nice of him to remember I wanted to read this. Come to think of it, he always used to buy me un-birthday presents – he just hasn't for a while. But he's less pressured at work now, so perhaps he's got more time for lunchtime shopping again.'

Or: 'Maybe he is feeling guilty about something. But

perhaps it's that he's been so busy we've hardly seen each other lately.'

Or: 'Perhaps he's picked up the growing distance between us. Perhaps this is his attempt to throw a rope bridge across the chasm. . . .'

You may need his help to understand what really lies behind his actions. You cannot discover what he's thinking by mind-reading. If you don't communicate with him, and explore *why* he has behaved a certain way – and simply *assume* that you know why – you may just persist in what could turn out to be quite a distorted perspective. Even a few attempts to discover *his* views of his actions might be quite illuminating, and it could lead to a re-evaluation on your part of what is going on.

Although distorted thinking won't always be a major problem, psychologists have developed what they call 'cognitive marital therapy' as one of a variety of therapeutic techniques to help couples in trouble. This involves getting couples to examine whether or not they have fallen into the habit of making faulty attributions – and also to check on any other types of distortions in thinking which may have made matters worse – and then working on them as necessary.

Distorted thinking

One of the founders of the whole approach called 'cognitive therapy' (used most extensively for treating depression and anxiety), the American psychiatrist Aaron Beck, has given some examples of problems in thinking:

Polarization. This is 'either-or' or 'all-or-nothing' thinking. If he's slightly less loving than usual, say, you panic and conclude that he doesn't love you any more.

Over-generalization. You make sweeping statements on the basis of a small number of events. 'If your spouse interrupts you, he or she "always" interrupts you. If your spouse shows some disrespect, he or she is "never" respectful.'

Tunnel vision. You pick out one detail of an experience, and screen out the rest. Let's say you are having a picnic by the river. You lean over to stroke his hand. He moves his hand away to scratch a freshly acquired gnat bite, and doesn't replace his hand under yours. You think: 'Oh, no! He's going off me.' The fact that the rest of the picnic involved laughing over the squashed egg mayonnaise sandwiches, chatting and giving each other periodic sloppy kisses is ignored, and the whole event is interpreted on the basis of that single detail.

Personalization. Considering yourself as the cause of your partner's behaviour when it's nothing whatsoever to do with you. 'He's in a vile mood. It must be because I splashed ketchup on his new jeans.'

Negative (global) labelling. This is where you apply a global, negative label to a person and not just to that person's actions. Beck gives examples: 'He is a weakling because he did not ask for a raise.' 'She is a nag because she wants me to quit drinking.'

Although you may decide that you need to seek relationships therapy, I do think it can be helpful at least to see the psychological thought traps we can fall into. To have a chance of scrambling out of them, we need to see what we're doing in the first place.

YOUR BEHAVIOUR HAS NOT CHANGED, BUT HE'S BECOME NEGATIVE

By now you can work out what I'm going to say. He may have changed in himself; he may be finding aspects of your relationship increasingly difficult; he may have fallen into distorted patterns of thinking about what *you* do. The only way to find out what's going on is to shine up those communication skills, take a huge brave breath and start asking.

You may conclude that you want some help.

THERAPY

Given what complex creatures relationships are, it's a very positive step if you choose to go for some outside assistance: to an organization like Relate (formerly the National Marriage Guidance Council), to chartered clinical or counselling psychologists with expertise in couples counselling, or to properly qualified marital therapists.

As I have said, such therapy or counselling is not guaranteed to 'work'. Indeed, what it may do is clarify the fact that the relationship cannot be saved. But this too you might find helpful in terms of moving forward in life – even if it is distressing for a period.

But counselling may help you both to get the relationship back on track. It may get you to start talking to each other. This may be a vital first step; marital therapists say that the most frequently experienced difficulty among couples who consult them is poor communication.

Indeed, talking is something you can start doing at any time. Often, trouble has occurred because you haven't been doing so. Maybe you thought, 'I've got him – I can relax now.' Or you've been together quite a long time, and perhaps complacency has crept in insidiously.

Many forces can combine to keep a couple in a relationship even if that relationship isn't going to well (not the best way to live one's life, I must say. . . .) For example: the other person might be seen as at least providing some sort of companionship and familiarity; there may be a fear of not finding anyone who'll be any better; feelings of moral obligation; you're both bound into a social network of relatives and mutual friends; you'll have financial and probably property ties; you've invested a great deal in the relationship (not least your time); and, very importantly, there may be children still living at home. There can be a risk, I think, that all these barriers to dissolving the relationship may sometimes lull people into a false sense of security. The relationship feels so buttressed that you take its stability for granted.

Researchers have pointed out that you may also be over-confident about your knowledge of your partner. Thinking that you know the other so well that you don't need to keep a weather eye on their state of mind is easily done. But it can be dangerous. You can lose sight of the other person *as a person*. It can become a habit to regard him as the occupant of a static role, as 'my partner' or 'only Pete', rather than as an individual with wants and needs and views of your relationship that can shift and change – and need to be monitored.

The best hope of repairing a relationship is to ask, in a non-threatening manner, what your partner is really thinking. If he is able to tell you, this at least means you can work out what – if anything – can be altered to bring the sparkle back for you both.

8

Recovering

With the best will in the world, relationships cannot always be saved – nor, in some cases, should they be. But when they do fall apart, it can be devastating. It will probably be worse if you are the one who's been left; but even if it's you who has done the leaving, you may suffer a lot of grief and guilt.

If you are about to enter – or have entered – this difficult period, take comfort. Even if you are feeling like hell now, and as if swarms of jaguars are lunching off your insides, the pain *will* ease in time. Cliché, but true. But you don't simply have to wait for time to pass; there are things you can do now to help yourself feel better.

CONSTRUCT A HELPFUL STORY

One of the most crucial ways to recover lies in the stories we construct about what has happened. Psychologists have pointed out that both parties to any break-up will develop an account of the relationship and of its collapse to tell both themselves and the outside world. Quite understandably, people want to make sense of it all; and they may well want to save face in front of their friends and relatives.

When I talk about 'stories', I don't mean that you make

something up about how he was abducted by a visiting Amazon queen on a short-hop flight to Manchester. But human beings do weave their past experiences into a story-like form, and often do a bit of reconstructing in the process. And as we know, so much interpretation is involved in trying to understand an upsetting event that a variety of plausible tales can be told about the same happening.

I think it is very important that your story should have several elements.

1 Most importantly, particularly if it's him who initiated the break-up, don't conclude that this means you are a ghastly, unlovable human being and it's all your fault. As I hope I have amply demonstrated, many relationships go wrong because they are so very complex to maintain and we don't always know how to do it. Or it may be that the two of you were insufficiently compatible from the outset. Or that you have grown apart and couldn't stop it. Or . . . . The point is that when relationships bite the dust this is usually because of what has been happening *between the two of you*. It does *not* mean you're a nightmare and should go and live alone in a cave and play with the bats. So concentrate your story on the dynamics of what happened, not on your worthlessness as a human being.

2 In order to save face, although you might in your heart of hearts feel (however irrationally) that it's your own doing, you may go to the other extreme and tell a tale in which it's all his fault. This, as I've said above, is almost certainly too simplistic. The trouble is that, unless of course it is strictly accurate, laying all the blame on him – although it might make you feel better for a bit – could hinder your learning process.

3 For you to get over this situation successfully and to get your relationships right in the future, you need to work out what might be learned from what has happened. You don't want to lose any vital lessons in relationships and in self-understanding which can be gained from all this pain.

It's true that relationships do sometimes break up because one of you has been behaving in a way the other finds intolerable. If that is the case, then what is to be learned may be very obvious and direct. Either (a) I will never behave like that again and I'll seek some professional help if I need it, or (b) I shall never again commit myself to someone who is, say, a total workaholic.

But the much more likely case, as I've said, is that something has gone awry in the way you interact. You need to focus your mind on those aspects. Once you've got a notion of what went wrong, that provides some sense of control. You are not at the mercy of cruel and unjust fate. Most vital of all, it should give you a feeling that, with care, *this need not happen again*. You can start to feel optimistic about the possibility of setting up future relationships with a better chance of success.

You may want to recruit his help – if that's possible. I believe that one of the greatest hindrances to recovery from a break-up is not really knowing what went wrong. It means you probably start to feel that relationship break-ups are out of your control; that you must be unlovable; that there's nothing to stop this pattern recurring; that no one will ever love you again.

All these devastating and untrue thoughts can be short-circuited by careful analysis (whether he's willing to help you with this or not) of your relationship and why it ended. Then you can learn whatever needs to be learned and – if not quite immediately, of course – move on.

Write about it

When you're feeling traumatized, and you haven't got your story straight in your head, here's a technique that might help. Write about it. But – not just anyhow.

American psychologist James Pennebaker has reviewed research on 'therapeutic writing' (mainly with students). He found that those who improved most in physical and psychological health tended to write in a certain way.

1 For about fifteen to twenty minutes over three or four days.
2 They used more negative emotional words – such as 'sad', 'hate', 'hurt', 'guilty' – than positive ones (e.g. 'happy', 'joy', 'peaceful').
3 Their use of words that showed insight and reflection (e.g. 'understand', 'realize', 'thought') and analysis of causes ('because', 'why', 'reason') increased from very low rates on the first day to high rates on the last.

The students who did *not* improve were much more positive in their writing and used 'insightful' words consistently over the few days. At first sight this looks very surprising. But they did not improve, the reviewer suggests, because they'd got a coherent story *too soon* in the writing process. They may not have properly confronted their traumatic experience. (Indeed, by the last day of writing, their stories were looking rather less coherent.)

The key to successful therapeutic writing is to use it to *develop* a coherent story over the writing days, and fully to express your bad feelings about what has happened. Then perhaps you can start to accept what's past – and to feel more optimistic.

BOOST YOUR SELF-ESTEEM

Despite your efforts with your break-up story, you may still feel that your self-esteem has taken rather a knock and currently feels the size of a walnut. The worse this break-up has made you feel about yourself, the harder it's going to be to recover. So you need to try to boost your self-esteem.

It may be that your self-esteem was pretty low before you even entered this relationship. What's more, your low self-esteem could have played its role in what has happened. It could have affected your choice of partner – to your detriment.

It's a strange idea that someone with low self-esteem might get together with a partner who doesn't think much of them either. But the evidence is that many of those who don't think highly of themselves prefer people who appraise them unfavourably. This seems very paradoxical. Why not choose someone who thinks well of you and try to make yourself feel better?

The main reason for negative-choosing-negative, according to American psychologist William Swann and his colleagues, seems to be that, if neither you nor the other person thinks a lot of you, then the other reassures you by confirming your self-view. Indeed, one study, they say, discovered that: 'When people with firmly held negative self-views find themselves with spouses who appraise them favourably, they tend to withdraw from the relationship.' People reported being more committed to a spouse the more that spouse made them feel 'that they really knew themselves'.

So in an attempt to have their social world feel more predictable and controllable, those who think badly of themselves may make choices that simply serve to maintain their low self-esteem. And if that relationship has now broken up, you're unlikely to be feeling very resilient.

Chronically low self-esteem

Psychologists define self-esteem as a global evaluation of oneself, ranging from positive to negative. Feeling that you're a pretty worthless, unlovable sort of person is one of the causes of, for example, depression, chronic jealousy, shyness and staying in relationships where you get treated badly. If you poke around in any of a whole welter of human miseries, the chances are that you'll find lurking, like the Beast in the Swamp, low self-esteem.

A chronic sense of worthlessness often stems from early experiences – feeling insufficiently loved by whoever looked after you, for example. But experiences at school can affect it, perceiving yourself as physically unattractive can feed into it; many experiences, in fact, can mould our self-esteem when young.

Our evaluation of ourselves isn't unalterable, however.

Good vs. bad qualities

A sensible first step is to start taking a more realistic view of yourself. All human beings have some good qualities and some faults. The trouble is that how well you think of yourself will affect how you *see* your good and bad points.

If you feel good about yourself, you will probably have a pretty sound idea of both your strengths and weaknesses, and you'll tend to evaluate the strengths as more important than the weaknesses. So you might know that, whenever you try to cook something special, all you can produce is a burned heap with watery bits round it. But you think: 'Well, at least my friends run to me with their troubles, and my latest report had the boss thrilled to his toupee. And cooking skills aren't all that vital anyway – what are frozen dinners for?'

But if you don't think well of yourself overall, you might just concentrate on your bad points. 'I don't cook, I incinerate; I have terrible legs; no one laughs at my jokes.' To make matters worse, you'll probably rate cooking, legs and wit as extremely important attributes.

To boost self-esteem, then, two strategies that can help are to focus more on your good points, while telling yourself how important they are; and to downgrade the importance of your negative ones. 'I am a bit impatient sometimes. But there are worse crimes . . . .'

Actual vs. ideal self

Our self-esteem comes partly from comparing our 'actual self' (as we see it) with our 'ideal self'. The bigger the gap, the more we think we're the pits. But it may well be, of course, that that ideal self is an unrealistic, super-genius, mega-stunning saint, whom any normal person would in fact loathe on sight.

We may also be comparing ourselves with other people in a way guaranteed to make us want to crawl under the duvet and stay there. Whom we compare ourselves with is one source of self-esteem, and if we constantly measure ourselves against, say, the (apparently) super-confident and successful, we do ourselves an injustice straightaway.

How often have you caught yourself looking at someone else and saying, 'Aaargh! Great legs, wit of Victoria Wood, socially at ease, handsome boyfriend. Duvet, here I come . . .'? A little exercise here might be to say things like: 'Well, yes. But I may be kinder, my nose is better, I've had devoted boyfriends in my time, and anyway lots of people like me – so what the hell!'

Helpful vs. unhelpful attributions

All this is not to say that yanking one's self-esteem up a few notches isn't a difficult business. The insidious danger of low self-esteem is that it has an ingenious way of perpetuating itself. So a person with such a feeling will tend to attribute successful events in all areas of life – acquisition of a new lover, praise for a project at work – to external circumstances. The acquisition of a new boyfriend will be put down to his need for a stronger pair of specs; the work success to the boss being in a good mood.

If a negative event happens to someone with low self-esteem, then they are prone to attributing it to some internal failure in themselves. 'My boyfriend's left me because why should he stay with a neurotic, fat ratbag like me?' 'The boss was cross with me because I'm no good at my job.'

Those with high – or indeed middling – self-esteem, on the other hand, are more prone to what psychologists call the 'self-serving bias'. That is, to protect or enhance their self-esteem, they put successes down to themselves and failures to external circumstances. Praise for a project at work: 'Yes, it was rather good, wasn't it? In-depth analyses of consumer petfood choices have always been one of my strong points, actually.' New boyfriend: 'Well, why not? I have my attractions, I guess. . . .'

But of life's googlies, interpretations are different. Boss critical: 'Gosh, he was in a bad mood. I bet head office have been nagging him abut expenses again.' Dumped by boyfriend: 'Not compatible, really. I should have suspected something when I discovered he thought culture was something you grew bugs in.'

Obviously, these are generalizations. Such differing interpretations are tendencies, not absolutes. Of course those with low self-esteem will sometimes take the credit for success and those with high self-esteem will sometimes take the blame for failure.

It is important to re-emphasize that self-esteem isn't a rigid entity. Psychologists see it as being a 'trait', in the sense that people do differ in their general levels of self-esteem; but it is also a 'state', in that external circumstances can raise or lower an individual's evaluation of themselves.

For those with low self-esteem, given its pervasive influence on one's life, it's worth tackling it head-on. A comforting point to realize is that a lot of people suffer from it. It's also worth noting that women are less likely than men to take the credit for success and more prone to blaming themselves for failure. Since such attributions contribute to one's global self-esteem, focusing on these is one method of raising it. Your feeling of self-worth will influence your reactions to many things in your life, not just your relationship break-up. To boost it, it might help to try to develop new habits of thought about what happens to you in *all* areas.

Shifting your attributions

One way of trying to shift your typical attributions is this: when something nice happens, write down your first thought about why it has come about. Under normal circumstances you might go no further and, having put this success down to factors outside yourself, rummage miserably in the fridge for a cream cake.

Instead, it may be illuminating to carry on thinking about other possible explanations and write them down. Maybe that man who's been chatting you up likes your sense of humour; maybe your report was really quite good; whatever. Then try to work out what the real cause – or causes – might have been. Sure, sometimes it won't have had much to do with you; but often, if you look at all the possible explanations realistically, you may see that perhaps you have had a bit of a hand in your success after all.

Similarly for nasty events. Maybe sometimes you should indeed take the blame, or some of it; but perhaps, if you try to explore all the possible causes, it might occur to you that external factors played a role. Yes, your boyfriend has gone to live with the woman who delivers the milk. But when you look closely, there are many elements which have played their part here. Not all awful events are the result of your 'awful self'.

Shifting the pattern of our attributions, psychologists find, can boost self-esteem. This can bring you a double benefit; it should help you in the recovery from the loss of your relationship, and might give you a better chance in the relationship stakes next time. Although research is in its early stages on this point, it does look as if, in long-term relationships, people want to verify their views of themselves. This implies that if you have higher self-esteem, you're more likely to choose a partner who thinks you're pretty good too – and this will help to maintain your more positive self-view.

To sum up, if you don't feel that wonderful about yourself, try:

1 Developing a clear picture of your good and bad points, and then concentrating more on your good ones and demoting the importance of your bad ones.
2 Not setting up an unrealistic 'ideal self'.
3 Not comparing yourself to the seemingly super-confident and successful (who may often simply be putting up an Oscar-winning performance in any case).

4 Examining *realistically* all the possible causes of your successes and failures in life, and not pressing the automatic self-denigration button.

It may sometimes be that your self-esteem is so low, and your self-destructive patterns of behaviour so ingrained, that some professional therapeutic help might be an excellent plan. I must say again: self-esteem *can be boosted* with practice and, if necessary, with help.

Temporarily knocked self-esteem

Even if your self-esteem was pretty healthy to start with, it may be feeling bruised in the aftermath of a relationship break-up. (Indeed, the latest evidence indicates that people can vary in how 'labile' their self-esteem is; that is, in how easily it rises and falls in response to outside events. It may be particularly labile if, for instance, you see your self-esteem as very much dependent on the opinion of significant other people in your life.) But the above advice should help your self-worth inflate too. In particular: focus on your good points; don't go round comparing yourself with people who seem to be blissfully happy in their relationships at this precise moment; and try to analyse as realistically as you can what went wrong.

Let's assume that you're working on your story and your self-esteem. What else can you do to dilute your emotional pain?

BELIEVE YOU CAN RECOVER

There is evidence that simply *believing* you have the ability to make yourself feel better is a significant element in itself.

American researchers Salvatore Catanzaro and Jack Mearns have devised a questionnaire to measure how strongly people expect they can do something to alleviate their negative moods. It consists of a statement, 'When I'm upset, I believe that . . .' followed by thirty different strategies for dealing with (or failing to deal with) your mood. For example, 'planning how I'll deal with things will help', 'wallowing in it is all I can do', and 'I can feel better by treating myself to something I like.' Respondents have to create to what extent they think each strategy generally will work for them.

Jack Mearns has gone on to use this questionnaire in a series of studies of the break-ups of romantic relationships among students. It transpires that those who think they *can* affect their moods actually feel less depressed in the first week following the collapse of their relationship.

Individuals who believe they can influence their feelings are also more likely to use 'active coping strategies'. These include things such as 'treated myself to something I like', 'tried to find out more about the situation', and 'made a plan of action and followed it'. Research shows that such strategies are more effective in relieving distress than is avoiding the issue by, say, refusing to believe it had happened or keeping things to yourself.

The researcher concludes that feeling you can regulate your own negative moods can *of itself* make you feel better when crunches come. As a bonus, it also results in people taking action in ways most likely to be effective in dealing with the strife.

And the heart-shattered certainly need to act. One of the studies showed that for those men and women who had experienced a break-up within the previous eight weeks, over 40 per cent were experiencing 'clinically measurable depression'. I'm sure we can all identify with that.

Let's look more closely at some actions you can take.

TAKE POSITIVE ACTION

When a relationship breaks up, it's quite easy to feel so miserable that you stay at home, hiding under the bedclothes and behind the answerphone.

Not a good move.

What you need at a time like this is some social support.

Seek social support

People sometimes feel humiliated, and go to ground because of that. But just about everyone has been through relationship break-ups, and all those who care for you are going to feel sympathy, not derision!

In the immediate aftermath of a break-up, what evidence there is indicates that turning to friends for support is more likely to help you than is quickly grabbing another man. (Of course, occasionally people do happily marry their rebounds; there are no rules, as I have said before. Research provides only generalizations, not predictions in individual cases. But it does provide clues to things to watch out for.) You may find that your ex, however, sees things differently. Women are often astonished – and sometimes offended – by the way their ex-partners behave after the split.

An American study by psychologist Kelly Sorenson and colleagues, of forty men and women aged between twenty and thirty-three, supports the idea that men and women cope differently after love has stubbed its toe. The women were more likely than the men to use 'confiding in good friends' as a restorative; the men were more prone than the women to use 'quickly starting to go out with others' as a means of recovery.

The researchers think there could be several reasons for this male tendency. First, men may feel a greater need to be in a relationship and try to move rapidly to replace a partner. This certainly fits with evidence that men have less intimate and confiding relationships with male (and female) friends that women do with women friends. So men may want another lover fast to obtain that sort of relationship.

Second (overlapping with the first), quick-daters may want someone to confide in about the loss of the previous relationship. Third, 'It also is possible that males who wish to preserve a strong masculine image may feel the need to show that they have not been hurt by a break-up and are able to pursue new relationships without emotional baggage.'

Quickly dating others may not, however, be a very effective coping mechanism. It was linked with suffering more severe physical symptoms, such as headaches and insomnia. The trouble is that such a strategy gives no time to work properly through thoughts and feelings about the relationship and why it ended.

Women seem more likely to give themselves that space. However, the evidence is that confiding in friends works best when friends are empathic and concerned. In this study, 55 per cent of the respondents said that friends and family had made things *worse*. The actions most often seen as impairing recovery were:

- suggesting that reconciliation was possible
- reminders by others of the former partner, such as having seen him or talking about him
- others *avoiding* talking about the ex-partner (obviously it's best to ask a heartbroken friend which they'd prefer: talk about him/her or not)
- others saying or doing things that lowered their self-esteem
- others avoiding talking to them at all

A *sensitive* pal, not a swift date, looks like a more effective stauncher of one's emotional blood.

So try to spend most time with those who make you feel better, not worse. You might not want to spend endless evenings with friends who tell you that they always thought he was a no-good rat, that it takes two weeks to get over these things, and that you should just pull yourself together.

Enhance your social life

The evidence is that having friends is good for our psychological and physical health. What can sometimes happen after a long-term relationship has ended, however, is that you look round and discover that you have let rather a lot of your old friends go.

You can do two things here. First, be brave, and ring them up. They may well be feeling that you had no use for them when you were happily in a relationship, and now he's gone you need them. This may, unfortunately, be the truth. So to have a chance of rectifying things, it might be best to come clean. Say you wish you hadn't let the friendship go, but you were so swept along in the rush of, let's say, marriage-plus-kids. You do regret it, and will never do it again even after you enter your next long-term relationship. After all, no one wants to feel used.

Some old friends will respond to this – others may not. But if you have friends you really would like to see again, aren't they worth a phone call?

The second thing you can do is try to meet some new people. Ask friends to introduce you to their friends, go out and about as much as you can, invite colleagues at work out for a drink, invite the neighbours in if you're at home with children, take up a new hobby which involves other people. Don't be afraid to make the first move; someone's got to, and the worst that can happen is that they'll say no (which you *would* survive). The best: a budding friendship.

If you're not feeling terribly sociable, or have never really regarded yourself as such, then you could try this. Decide that, at the next social event you attend, you're going to present yourself to everyone as really friendly and outgoing. Psych yourself up by thinking of times when you were in an extremely good mood and felt terrific about yourself.

Research from America shows what real effects this can have. After students had been interviewed in that frame of mind, compared to others who weren't interviewed:

- they rated themselves as more sociable
- when left in a waiting room with someone (secretly a confederate of the researchers), they behaved more

sociably in this situation as well. They spoke sooner, more frequently and for a longer time; and were rated as more sociable by the confederate too.

Behaving very sociably in the interview had shifted the students' view of themselves. Even more crucially, it also affected how they behaved afterwards – and others' reactions to them – which might go on to influence their self-view even more.

After all, other people are more likely to warm to you if you appear to like them and, evidence indicates, are more sociable, animated and positive than the reverse. These warm responses might help to boost your self-esteem and sociability – and set you off on a cheering upward spiral.

The enhancement to your life of having a richer social whirl could be immense.

Friendship skills

We all probably have one or two friends who aren't, frankly, terribly good at the job. It isn't that they're not fond of us, but they don't seem to know quite how to *be* a friend. Being a friend takes skill and, as with love relationships, friendships need to be developed and then kept polished. So, partly based on research on friendship by British social psychologists Michael Argyle and Monika Henderson, here are a few ideas:

Don't

- listen to their troubles and say, 'Yes, I know what you mean, let me tell you what's been happening to *me. . . .*'
- talk in long monologues, and when your friend manages to insert a sentence say, 'Yes, but . . .' and carry on in an unstoppable wave
- say bitchy things about your friend's failings/recent disastrous choices in the man department to mutual friends (it will get back to your friend and get you a bad reputation with the mutual friends)

- only ring them when you're in trouble
- always expect *them* to ring *you* to make arrangements to meet
- nag
- flirt with their partners
- be jealous or intolerant of their other friends
- tell them their beloved is a toe rag
- listen to their confidences, then rush to the phone and start dialling
- only arrange to see them when your current man is out of town and you're at a loose end
- give them anti-wrinkle cream for Christmas

Do

- offer help when they've got problems
- stand up for them in their absence
- ring *them* up occasionally to see how they are/fix a meeting
- make sure you do actually have some happy times together, not just endless misery-exchanging sessions
- give them 50 per cent of the conversational airtime
- share your good news as well as your problems
- if you feel they're making a bad mistake, gently give them your opinion and then unswervingly stand by them if they continue to make it — and stock up on Kleenex
- just now and again, let them know how much you value their friendship

With those friends who do help in the aftermath of your break-up, you might worry that you're going to drive them away because you are so miserable. What I'd advise here is to get everything off your chest on, say, the first two or three occasions you meet them after the crash. After that, although you need to feel free to be able to refer to it when you want, try to allocate increasing proportions of your evenings to-gether to other topics: to what's going on in your friend's life, to the latest royal scandal, to your leaking lavatory, whatever. You need to regain a sense that life goes on, and is a rich and unpredictable business.

You need, too, to provide some friendship rewards to the other person. Of course it's true that a real friend will put up with an immense amount of shoulder-wetting. But in the end, they'll need some return – and being allowed to weep without ceasing may in the end not be doing you any favours. You also need friends to say, 'Let's go out and *do* something that we'll both get pleasure from.'

This will help by stopping you ruminating and by focusing your mind on enjoyable activities.

Increase and widen your activities

Don't ruminate

If you're feeling low and can't seem to shake it off, you may be using what psychologists call 'ruminative coping'. That is, you're focusing on your feelings of depression, and their possible causes and consequences. For instance, you think about how sad you feel, wonder why you always react this way, worry about what it means that you feel like this and what'll happen if you don't get over it. You're 'staying with' your emotions rather than taking action to lift the mood. Research by American psychologist Susan Nolen-Hoeksema and her colleagues has found that this prolongs depression; and that women are more prone to doing it than men.

What may be happening, the researchers think, is that women see themselves as being 'naturally emotional' or 'in touch with their emotions' more than men do. This may be absolutely fine, except when those emotions are sad ones and your self-image leads you to concentrate on them. Then you might just fuel your misery.

You need to walk rather a slender emotional tightrope. Suppressing your emotions isn't a good idea, because that can make it harder to adjust to upsetting experiences. (What's more, the researchers say, people who try to suppress their feelings may end up ruminating on them even more.) On the other hand, you don't want to wallow endlessly in them either.

So let your emotions out *and* practise some distraction techniques. The researchers list a few:

- do something you enjoy
- think of something to make yourself feel better
- do something active to get your mind off your feelings
- go to a favourite place to distract yourself
- do something fun with a friend
- concentrate on something other than how you feel

You don't want your female pride in your emotions to yank you into the depths and keep you there.

Increase enjoyable activities

That 'do something you enjoy' suggestion is an important one. A well-known technique for inducing a positive mood is to make a list of activities you find highly pleasurable, even if you haven't done them for quite some time. This can be anything at all: reading trashy novels, visiting stately homes, going to concerts, seeing your friends, playing tennis, spending time with your children. (Don't get carried away here, though – some activities might be bad for you or for other people. Cross off ideas of the 'eating a huge box of chocolates all in one go' ilk.) Having compiled your list, make a conscious effort to indulge in each of these activities more often.

You'd probably be surprised at how little time you have been spending on doing things which might make you feel better. Watching funny films and reading cheerful stories, for instance, have both been found to be effective at improving people's mood. Obviously, no technique will always work for everyone. But making a conscious effort to increase the time you spend on activities you revel in has at least a chance of doing so.

If you're feeling as though your insides have been ripped out with red-hot pincers, and you keep soaking your pillowcases and wish you'd bought shares in a tissue company – well, isn't anything worth a go?

Explore new activities

It may be that, without the relationship which has now gone, you can explore some new things. Either because you have more time, or because there's no one there saying, 'What do you want to do that for?' Perhaps there are subjects you've always been interested in, or activities you've always wished to attempt, or even a new type of job you've wanted to try or train for. There may, of course, be some practical limitations on what you can do, perhaps because you have young children and/or you've had to deal with a drop in income.

Adjusting to a change in your financial circumstances is a new, unwanted activity that you may, unfortunately, have to do. This is a common fate, unfairly, for women (and sometimes men) left as single parents. It falls outside the scope of this book; but there are books available which cover just this sort of issue, and you can seek advice from friends as well as relevant professionals. Taking action in a thorough and positive way will improve your sense of control over what's happening, as well as being likely to lead to more satisfactory practical outcomes for you.

But despite any current practical limitations, you may find that it is still possible to try something new that you *do* want to do; and that this might help you. It could cheer you up, engage your interest, bring you new friends, boost your self-esteem, maybe even provide a potential new source of income. If you've always secretly wanted to train to be a motor mechanic or study French or become an expert house-plant tender – well, could this be your opportunity?

CHILDREN

If you and your ex-partner have children, you may be particularly worried at this time about the effects of the break-up on them. This may be exacerbated by shock-horror media head-lines of the 'divorce is bad for your kids' variety.

These are derived from comparing children of divorced parents with children whose parents are still together. The statistics show that in various ways – such as schoolwork, social behaviour and so on – the children of divorces, on average, do worse.

But the crucial thing to realize here is that these are *average differences between groups*. So if, say, 5 per cent of adults brought up by both parents have psychiatric difficul-ties, the rate will be about 6 or 7 per cent among adults whose parents separated when they were children. Although there may be more children with a particular problem in the 'divorced' group, many children will not have that problem. Any potential bad effects of divorce are *not* inevitable.

So what can you do to minimize the effects on your own children? Researchers have found two factors to be particu-larly important. Children do better if:

- they maintain a good relationship with both their mother and father
- they are not exposed to conflict between their parents

So however churned up you may be feeling about what has happened, it's important that the children should be able to see the non-resident parent, who is often the father (unless, obviously, he poses a danger to them). Any conflict between the two of you needs to be conducted out of their sight. Nor should they be drawn in as pawns in your conflict.

It could also help them if you sat them down and told them properly what was happening, and why. Children, researchers find, are often not given an adequate explanation, and are left bewildered. They may even feel guilty, thinking 'If I hadn't been so naughty/difficult, Dad might not have left.' they need to be reassured that it was nothing to do with them.

It's also important to keep in touch with how they are

feeling; it would help them to be encouraged to talk. Their teachers at school will need to be informed, so that they too can keep their eye on the children and let you know if they are starting to behave unusually (perhaps becoming aggressive, or withdrawn) or if their schoolwork is getting worse. You may need to seek some counselling for your children during this difficult period of adjustment. The school may have a counsellor attached to it; or your GP should be able to find someone to help if necessary.

For your own sake as well as your children's, you too may need help to resolve conflicts with your ex-partner. Mediation and conciliation services, for example, may be available and are certainly worth considering. This could help you work out the practicalities of the situation when you feel in a very heightened emotional state.

It may be, too, that you need some outside assistance with that emotional state. I have suggested ways which might help you through the painful period after a break-up. But if you feel that nothing is working and your anguish is going on and on and you can't bear it, then look for some help yourself. Relate offers counselling in the aftermath of relationship break-ups, and there are others – qualified chartered psychologists, therapists and counsellors – who can help too. There really is no need to flounder endlessly in pain and pessimism. The future may look black at this moment; but with time and effort on your part, it can transform to a vista of unknown and exciting possibilities.

STARTING AGAIN

In the fullness of time, you will probably want to commit yourself again. Often people say, 'Ah, but the divorce rate for second marriages is higher than for first ones.' This may be because, if things go wrong the second time, people find it easier to seek a divorce having done it once already. But there may be other elements too. It can be hard to be a step-parent, for instance. (There are books devoted to this topic alone: see Further Reading.) Perhaps some people marry (or seriously commit themselves) the second time round for the wrong reasons: panic, fear of loneliness, wanting a fast substitute parent for their children.

It's better to use periods on your own to develop areas of your life that will always stand you in good stead. Perhaps developing your work, or starting a new type of work; building up your friendships; exploring new aspects of yourself, your interests and talents. Then when you meet someone special again, you can go into a new relationship in a stronger and more clear-eyed fashion. You can also go into it more knowledgeably, thus giving yourself a better chance of getting what you deserve out of the whole love business – a good, fulfilling relationship that will last. Which brings us back to Chapter 1 . . .

Whether your goal is a long-standing commitment or a marriage, knowing more about the complexities of relationships can, I believe, do nothing but good. Of course, a relationship is between two people, and you do not bear the whole responsibility for how it turns out. But you can pass on what you learn to current or future partners too – and perhaps the apparent vagaries of love will come to seem not quite so inexplicable after all. More importantly, they should come to seem rather more controllable. You can do a great deal to give yourself and your partner a smoother sail through what are – as we all know – potentially choppy seas. I wish you a happy journey, and hope you find this book a useful anti-storm device.

Further reading

Horley, S. (1988) *Love and Pain: A survival handbook for women*, Bedford Square Press

Lewis, S. and Cooper, C.L. (1989) *Career Couples: Contemporary lifestyles and how to manage them*, Unwin

Litvinoff, S. (1993) *The Relate Guide to Starting Again*, Vermilion

Marshall, P. (1994) *Cinderella Revisited: How to survive your stepfamily without a fairy godmother*, BPS Books (British Psychological Society)

Tysoe, M. (1992) *Love Isn't Quite Enough: The psychology of male-female relationships*, Fontana

Where to go for help

If your relationship is in trouble, or if you need help to recover from the break-up of a relationship, or want advice on personal/sexual problems, you could contact any of the following organisations.

British Association for Counselling
1 Regent Palace
Rugby CV21 2PJ
Telephone (information line): 01788 578328

Provides a comprehensive list of accredited counsellors in your area and a free fact sheet about counselling

National Family Mediation
9 Tavistock Place
London WC1H 9SN
Telephone: 0171 383 5993

Sixty centres nationwide, providing support and help in making arrangements for children

National Council for Divorced and Separated
NCDS
13 High Street
Little Shelford
Cambridge CB2 5ES
Telephone: 01533 700595

115 branches nationwide, providing social gatherings for single agains

Relate (formerly the National Marriage Guidance Council)
Herbert Gray College
Little Church Street
Rugby CV21 3AP
Telephone: 01788 573241

Will see you on your own or with your partner, and charge only according to your means. For your nearest branch, look in your local phone book. For further information, contact the headquarters at the above address

Relationships Australia
15 Napier Close
Deakin Act 2600
Australia
Telephone: (00 61) 06 285 4466

Westminster Pastoral Foundation
23 Kensington Square
London W8 5HN
Telephone: 0171 937 6956

Offers an excellent counselling service to a wide range of people with various problems. Also has associated counselling services in many parts of the country.

Women's Therapy Centre
629 Manor Gardens
London N7 6LA
Telephone: 0171 263 6200

Offers advice and information to women with all sorts of difficulties and problems, including sexual issues

You could also consult *The Directory of Chartered Psychologists*, published by the British Psychological Society. This should be available in your main local public reference library. The directory includes lists of the names and addresses of many chartered clinical psychologists and chartered counselling psychologists. These are indexed by geographical location and by specialism, so you can see if there is a chartered psychologist in your area who specialises in your personal problem and/or in relationship difficulties. Each person's details will mention whether the person works in private practice and/or in the NHS. (Normally you would have to be referred to an NHS psychologist – whose services will be free – by your GP.) Chartered psychologists have passed the stringent qualifications and entry requirements laid down by the British Psychological Society and are subject to a code of conduct, so you can be certain that you would be seeing a professional who is fully and appropriately qualified. For further help or information, contact:

The British Psychological Society
St Andrews House
48 Princess Road East
Leicester LE1 7DR
Telephone: 0116 254 9568

Index

Index

lovemaps, 6–7

marriage
  no-love motives for, 31
  reluctance to commit to, 31–
    42
  et passim
Martin, Robert, 161
matching physical
    attractiveness, 9
Mearns, Jack, 186–7
menopause, 155
Miell, Dorothy, 93, 111
Mikulincer, Mario, 36
mind-reading, 46, 47
misrepresentation, 10–11
Money, John, 6
mothers, childhood
    relationships with, 35
motives, 18–19

Nadler, Arie, 126
negative labelling, distorted
    thinking, 174
negative moods
  belief in recovery, 186–7
  boosting self-esteem, 180–6
neuroticism, 46
Nolen-Hoeksema, Susan, 193

Olson, David, 50
orgasm, 144
O'Sullivan, Lucia, 132

parents, partner's similarity to,
    6–7
partner's perspective, taking,
    96–8
Pennebaker, James, 179

personalization, distorted
    thinking, 174
perspective, partner's, 96–8
physical attractiveness,
    matching, 9
physical violence, 45, 71–3
polarization, distorted thinking,
    173
post-natal depression, 109–10
potential partners, 3–22
  being in love, 19–22
  motives, 18–19
  self-deception, 11–17
  sexual attraction, 6–9
  similarity, 9–11
  snap judgements, 3–5
powering, 75–101
  common rewards, 82–8
  expressions of love, 83–8, 90
  fairness, 81–2
  lifestyle, 88–96
  rewards and costs, 76–81
problems, repairing, 157–76

quarrels *see* conflict

recovering from a break-up,
    177–98
  believing in recovery, 186–7
  boosting self-esteem, 180–6
  children and, 195–7
  increasing activities, 193–5
  new activities, 195
  quick dating, 188–9
  social support, 188–93
  starting again, 197–8
  story of events, 177–80
  taking positive action, 187–
    95
  writing about, 179–80
Relate, 175, 197, 200

Piatkus Books

If you have enjoyed reading this book, you may like to read other titles published by Piatkus.
These include:

Social Topics & Popular Psychology

Adult Children of Divorce: How to achieve happier relationships
Dr Edward W. Beal and Gloria Hochman

Art As Medicine: Creating a therapy of the imagination
Shaun McNiff

At My Father's Wedding: Reclaiming our true masculinity
John Lee

Children of Alcoholics: How a parent's drinking can affect your life
David Stafford

The Chosen Child Syndrome: What to do when a parent's love rules your life
Dr Patricia Love and Jo Robinson

Codependents' Guide to the Twelve Steps: How to understand and follow a recovery programme
Melody Beattie

Codependency: How to break free and live your own life
David Stafford and Liz Hodgkinson

Creating Love: The next stage of growth
John Bradshaw

Dare to Connect: How to create confidence, trust and loving relationships
Susan Jeffers

Don't Call It Love: Recovery from sexual addiction
Patrick Carnes

Father-Daughter Dance, The: Insight, inspiration and understanding for every woman and her father
Barbara Goulter and Joan Minninger

Fire in the Belly: On being a man
Sam Keen

Growing Old Disgracefully: New ideas for getting the most out of life
The Hen Co-Op

He Says, She Says: Closing the Communication gap between the sexes
Dr Lillian Glass

Homecoming: Reclaiming and championing your inner child
John Bradshaw

Journey from Lost to Found, The: The search that begins with the end of a relationship
Susan Jeffers

Obsessive Love: How to free your emotions and live again
Liz Hodgkinson

Off the Hook: How to break free from addiction and enjoy a new way of life
Corinne Sweet

Opening Our Hearts to Men: Taking charge of our lives and creating a love that works
Susan Jeffers

The Passion Paradox: What to do when one person loves more than the other
Dr Dean C. Delis with Cassandra Phillips

Protect Yourself! A Woman's Handbook: How to be safer in the streets, in the home, at work, when travelling
Jessica Davies

The Second Shift: Working parents and the revolution at home
Dr Arlie Hochschild

Tao of Negotiation, The: How to resolve conflict in all areas of your life
Joel Edelman and Mary Beth Crain

Total Confidence: The complete guide to self-assurance and personal success
Philippa Davies

When Food is Love: Exploring the relationship between eating and intimacy
Geneen Roth

Women and Guilt: How to set aside your feelings of guilt and lead a positive life
Ursula Markham

Health & Healing

Healing Breakthroughs: How your attitudes and beliefs can affect your health
Dr Larry Dossey

Hypnosis Regression Therapy: How reliving your early experiences can improve your life
Ursula Markham

**Increase Your Energy: Regain your zest for life the
natural way**
Louis Proto

**Nervous Breakdown: What is it? What causes it? Who
can help?**
Jenny Cozens

**Personal Growth Handbook, The: Dozens of ways to
develop your inner self**
Liz Hodgkinson

**Picture of Health, The: How to use guided imagery for
self-healing and personal growth**
Helen Graham

Qigong for Health & Vitality
Michael Tse

Self-Healing: Use your mind to heal your body
Louis Proto

Stress Control Through Self-Hypnosis
Dr Arthur Jackson

**Your Healing Power: A comprehensive guide to channel-
ling your healing energies**
Jack Angelo

New Age – Mind, Body & Spirit

**Awakening to Change: A guide to self-empowerment in
the new milennium**
Soozi Holbeche

**Be Your Own Best Friend: How to achieve greater self-
esteem and happiness**
Louis Proto

**Care of the Soul: How to add depth and meaning to your
everyday life**
Thomas Moore

Creating Abundance: How to bring wealth and fulfilment into your life
Andrew Ferguson

Inward Bound: Exploring the geography of your emotions
Sam Keen

Living Magically: A new vision of reality
Gill Edwards

Mindfulness Meditation for Everyday Life
Jon Kabat-Zinn

Power and Inner Peace, The
Diana Cooper

Rituals for Everyday Living: Special ways of marking important events in your life
Lorna St Aubyn

Saved by the Light: The true story of a man who died twice and the profound revelations he received
Dannion Brinkley with Paul Perry

Stepping into the Magic: a new approach to everyday life
Gill Edwards

Teach Yourself to Meditate: Over 20 simple exercises for peace, health and clarity of mind
Eric Harrison

Transformed by the Light: The powerful effect of near-death experiences on people's lives
Dr Melvin Morse with Paul Perry

Transform Your Life: A step-by-step programme for change
Diana Cooper

Sex

Becoming Orgasmic
Julia R. Heiman and Joseph LoPiccolo

**Good Vibrations: The complete guide to sex aids and
erotic toys**
Suzie Hayman

**Hot Monogamy: How to achieve a more intimate rela-
tionship with your partner**
Dr Patricia Love and Jo Robinson

**Nice Couples Do: How to make your sexual fantasies
come true**
Joan Elizabeth Lloyd

For a free brochure with our complete list of titles,
please write to:

Piatkus Books
Freepost 7 (WD 4505)
London W1E 4EZ

PIATKUS